DOWN SIZING

MADE SIMPLE

RACHEL LANE
NOEL WHITTAKER

NWH

Other titles by Rachel Lane and Noel Whittaker:
AGED CARE, WHO CARES?
RETIREMENT LIVING HANDBOOK

Other titles by Noel Whittaker:

MAKING MONEY MADE SIMPLE
MORE MONEY WITH NOEL WHITTAKER
GOLDEN RULES OF WEALTH
SHARES MADE SIMPLE
BORROWING TO INVEST
SUPERANNUATION MADE SIMPLE
BEGINNER'S GUIDE TO WEALTH
10 SIMPLE STEPS TO FINANCIAL FREEDOM

GETTING IT TOGETHER
LIVING WELL IN RETIREMENT
CONTROLLING YOUR CREDIT CARDS
DRIVING SMALL BUSINESS
LOANS MADE SIMPLE
MONEY TIPS
25 YEARS OF WHITT & WISDOM
RETIREMENT MADE SIMPLE

Also, by Noel Whittaker and Julia Hartman:
WINNING PROPERTY TAX STRATEGIES

DOWNSIZING MADE SIMPLE
First published in Australia in 2019 by Noel Whittaker Holdings Pty Ltd

Visit our website at *www.downsizingmadesimple.com.au*

© Rachel Lane and Noel Whittaker Holdings Pty Ltd 2023

A catalogue record for this book is available from the National Library of Australia

ISBN 978-0-6458216-5-9 (pbk)

Editing by Helena Bond
Cover design & typesetting by Sharon Felschow, dta studio
Front cover image all-free-download.com (modified)
Cartoons by Paul Lennon
Printed in Australia by McPhersons Printing Group, Victoria

Dedicated to senior Australians. You have played a major part in building this great country, and we hope that this book will help you seize the opportunity to enjoy the golden years of your life.

ABOUT THE AUTHORS

RACHEL LANE explains retirement living and aged care like no-one else. She breaks down complex financial arrangements into plain and engaging English, empowering people to understand the pros and cons of their options.

For almost 20 years Rachel has specialised in the financial planning aspects of retirement. Over that time she has also assisted her grandmother — affectionately known as "Ducky", and the source of many stories — to navigate her way through a retirement village, a home care package, a few respite stays and more recently a move to an aged care home. Rachel holds a Masters in Financial Planning, and through her many years' professional and personal experience has become known as "the aged care guru".

As Principal of Aged Care Gurus, Rachel oversees a national network of specialist financial advisers. She recently created "Village Guru", a software program that demystifies the financial aspects of moving to a retirement community.

She is highly sought after as a presenter at conferences and seminars across the country, writes regular columns for newspapers, magazines and websites, and often speaks on radio and television.

NOEL WHITTAKER is an international bestselling author, finance and investment expert, radio broadcaster, newspaper columnist and public speaker; he is one of the world's foremost authorities on personal finance.

Noel reaches over seven million readers each week through his columns in major Australian newspapers in Sydney, Melbourne, Perth and Brisbane. He contributes to magazines and websites, and appears on radio and television.

Noel is one of Australia's most successful authors, with 23 bestselling books achieving worldwide sales of more than two million copies. His first book, *Making Money Made Simple*, set Australian sales records, was named in the 100 Most Influential Books of the Twentieth Century and is now in its twenty-third edition.

For 30 years, Noel was a Director of Whittaker Macnaught, one of Australia's leading financial advice companies, with more than two billion dollars under management. He relinquished all interests in that business in 2007.

In 2003, he was awarded the Australian Centenary Medal in recognition of his services to the financial services industry, and in 2011 he was made a Member of the Order of Australia for service to the community in raising awareness of personal finance.

Noel is now an Adjunct Professor and Executive-in-Residence with the Queensland University of Technology and a member of the Australian Securities and Investment Commission (ASIC) consumer liaison committee.

ACKNOWLEDGEMENTS

Writing a book is a bit like building a substantial financial portfolio. It takes time, and the assistance of people who can help you along the way.

First, we give a very special thanks to our readers who shared their downsizing experiences in the hope that it made someone else's decisions easier and to our proofreaders Anne Lane, Jemma Briscoe and Geraldine Whittaker.

We are indebted to the following experts for their generous input in their specialist areas. Frank Higginson and Michael Teys for the strata title chapter, Caitlin McGee for collaborative housing, Robin Lyons for retirement community contracts, and Julia Hartman for the tax issues on granny flats.

Special thanks go to our editor, Helena Bond, who always goes the extra mile in her work, and to Sharon Felschow, who has been typesetting our books for 20 years. Paul Lennon has done a great job on the cartoons once again and McPhersons, as usual, have taken care of the printing.

You are all a great team!

CONTENTS

EXERCISES

INTRODUCTION

In *Downsizing Made Simple*, we want to guide you through the maze to a future that works for you. After a lifetime of contribution, you surely deserve to find your golden years.

Part 1 explores the choices you'll need to make to decide whether downsizing is for you, and how you might fund a change. With exercises, calculators and checklists to help put your own situation into the frame, you'll gain a clearer understanding of your options — and their pros and cons.

Part 2 focuses on where you are going to next: demystifying strata title homes, granny flats, other collaborative housing options, and purpose-designed retirement communities, with the wide range of legal and financial arrangements that may apply. We share case studies that shed light on both financial and emotional aspects of moving. And we'll let you in on a secret right now: we often hear people say their only regret is that they didn't downsize sooner. So don't be one of the pack: get clear and get going.

In **Part 3**, we explain how to navigate getting care in your own home, and outline residential aged care too, so you can plan ahead. In doing so, we bust a few myths, clarify what services exist and the timelines involved, and show you how to access good quality, good value care.

Grab a paper and pen, pour your favourite drink, and explore your future with us.

PART 1:

IS IT TIME TO DOWNSIZE?

Many people spend a significant portion of their lives creating their "forever" home, so it can come as a shock to discover that it is time to move on. While leaving often feels like the big decision, really, deciding where to go next is much more important.

There are lots of reasons why people decide to downsize. Some have an urge for a "sea change" or a "tree change" — a different pace of life — some want a low maintenance home while remaining in their current neighbourhood, some want to move closer to family or friends, some want to be more connected socially, and some are seeking luxury.

For many people, downsizing is about paying off any remaining debt, freeing themselves from endless maintenance on house and garden (no more ladders!), having lower bills and more time to spend doing the things they love. It can also be about freeing up some equity to invest, or spend, or a bit of both.

Unlike when you "upsize" your home, perhaps when you were searching for a 3 or 4 bedroom home to accommodate a growing family, when you "downsize" (or "rightsize" as we prefer to call it) you will find that there is a smorgasboard of options available to you. You may like to move to a new freehold home, a strata-title apartment or townhouse, a retirement village or land lease community, or perhaps a granny flat or collaborative housing arrangement.

It's important not to neglect the financial aspects: what you do and how you go about it can make downsizing a financially positive move — or a financial disaster. Your choices can have wide ranging financial implications for things like how much money you will have to spend or invest, how much age pension (and other benefits) you can receive, the cost of a home care package, the amount of money left to your estate, and if your next move is to an aged care home, your ability to fund that.

You'll find several exercises in this part to help you work through your options. There are exercises to help you decide on the home, location and lifestyle that best suit you, calculators to help you understand the costs, and exercises and checklists so you are clear on the legal aspects of your new home.

1

KNOW YOUR WHY

Whenever you move house, there are decisions to make. You've done this before, and you can do it again. With a lifetime of making decisions behind you, you know that there is no right, wrong or best when it comes to downsizing: there is only the choice that best suits you. So let's get started with an exercise.

Ask yourself these questions to complete *Exercise 1*:

1. What do you want to leave behind? What irritates you about your current home? Why do you want to go? Write these in the "leave" column.
2. What do you love about your home? What are the things you want to keep? Write these in the "keep" column.
3. What do you hope for in your new home? What draws you to make a move? How do you want your new place to support your future? Write these in the "change" column.

EXERCISE 1: *Why move?*

Leave	Keep	Change

If you need more space, draw your own columns on any piece of paper, or download a smart PDF to print or type into from www.downsizingmadesimple.com.au.

Location, location, location

Where you live affects how you live, and it's one thing you can't change without moving again. You might have realised that you long for a "sea change" or a "tree change" … you might crave a more luxurious lifestyle wherever you go, or simply want a smaller place close to your current home.

You know yourself. If you dream of spending hours walking along a secluded beach or days in the mountains reading a book in front of an open fire, are these things you will actually do? As you age, are your desires changing? How about your physical capabilities? As Shakespeare put it: "to thine own self be true"…

Do you want to be near friends and family? You may want to move closer — or further away from — certain people. Of course, for some people, proximity to family is an almost impossible feat, with children and grandchildren spread right across the country or the world

— though you might choose to be near an international airport if you want frequent visitors. And if you do, you may need a larger apartment or unit to accommodate the regular flow of people.

What about the conveniences around you? Do you want to be close to places where people gather? Will the noise annoy you? Would you rather be away from the action, where it is a little more peaceful?

And the question you may have been avoiding: what about proximity to care and medical services? You may be fit and active right now, but if that ever changes — if you are like the vast majority of people — you will want to stay at home, in the place you know and love. The industry calls this "ageing in place". If this is what you would like, then ask the question: what would happen if I needed care?

If you do need care — whether temporary, perhaps to recover from an operation, or ongoing — it's important to know how you would access those services and what they would cost. Many newer homes, particularly those in retirement communities, are built with a view to delivering care in the future. If this is on your checklist, make sure you ask about the options, and check for things as you choose your new accommodation that may make delivery of care difficult, like narrow doorways and pokey bathrooms.

Now, let's get those thoughts on paper.

EXERCISE 2: Location, location, location

Near	Far	Not important to me

If you need more space, draw your own columns on any piece of paper, or download a smart PDF to print or type into from www.downsizingmadesimple.com.au.

Next take some time to think about what activities you enjoy doing or are hoping to enjoy doing. Few people plan to spend their lives in an easy chair watching television, but if you don't plan anything else, you may find that's what you end up doing. And consider whether you like to spend most of your time on your own, with your partner, or with a group of people … Most of us need to get out and about every day to maintain our mental health and social ties.

If you are looking at retirement communities, in almost every brochure you will see the word "lifestyle", yet every community is different. Bear in mind that the more facilities and activities the village provides the higher the on-going service charges are likely to be. This isn't necessarily a problem if you are using and enjoying these things, but if you're not, you are still paying for them. A good way to see what is on offer is to get hold of the community's social calendar and highlight the activities you would like to participate in.

It's not that different in a local community, except that all the ratepayers are helping to fund activities and facilities, and they won't all be targeted at your age group. You want activities to be there when you are interested, and to be able to retreat to your unit, or to a communal lounge or library, when you want time to relax. In a retirement village you know you won't be chased out by "young hooligans", but you may long for the vibe that comes from having children, teens, and adults of all ages living together.

Jot down your ideas about the things you want to stop doing, start doing, or keep on with in *Exercise 3*.

EXERCISE 3: Lifestyle choices

Stop	Start	Keep doing

*If you need more space, draw your own columns on any piece of paper, or download a smart PDF to print or type into from **www.downsizingmadesimple.com.au**.*

Choose your own adventure

You have an amazing range of options available to you. You may want to buy a new freehold home; move into a strata title apartment or townhouse; choose a retirement community; explore a mobile home; or establish a granny flat or other collaborative living arrangement.

Remember, there is no right, wrong or best when it comes to downsizing decisions. There is only the one that best suits you.

The accommodation itself is an important consideration, though we often tell people not to get too hung up on floor plans and colour schemes. You will need to think about what spaces you need. For some couples, for example, his snoring or her desire to watch late-night TV may mean that a minimum of two bedrooms so one can escape to a comfortable bed rather than a couch is an important consideration.

Let's have a look at the key types of accommodation and their features.

TABLE 1: *Accommodation options*

Accommodation type	Features
Granny flat	Often thought of as a self-contained dwelling in the backyard of someone else's home but it can be part of an existing home.
Townhouse	Typically 2–3 storeys high, often with shared "party walls" (the wall of your house is also the wall for the house next door).
Unit / Apartment / Flat	Typically, a single-level dwelling within a multi-level building that consists of other apartments, and may include communal facilities such as a lobby or gym, and/or retail facilities such as a café.
Duplex / Semi-detached home	Two homes built as a pair with a party wall down the middle separating the two.
Mobile home	A caravan or a houseboat is clearly a mobile home, but others that you may not think of, such as the homes in a land lease community, can also technically be mobile. Of course, moving one of these homes is far more involved than connecting it to a tow bar on your car.

What exactly will you be signing?

You will need to sign some sort of contract, whether you are buying your new home freehold/strata title; entering into a leasehold/licence arrangement in a retirement community; or establishing a granny flat arrangement.

The role of a contract is to set out your rights, responsibilities and costs. Your job is to work out if the contract represents what you think is a fair balance of those three things. The thing with contracts is that once they are signed they are rarely looked at until the unexpected happens and people are not sure of what to do or what their rights are in this situation.

Your contract is *really* important. It will have many consequences for: your pension entitlement; eligibility for rent assistance; money available to invest; ability to afford the lifestyle you want now and in the future; and — if the need arises — your financial position in accessing and affording aged care.

A granny flat, in particular, can be tricky. It is not "arm's length", may not be on commercial terms, and if it goes wrong the fallout is likely to impact the whole family. Nonetheless, it is vital that you have a contract: things can get so much worse if you don't.

Create a table for each of the options you are considering. This can help make sure you don't focus on just one element of the contract. Breaking it down into three time zones, before you move in, while you live there and when you leave, can also help identify exactly what happens when.

EXERCISE 4: *Accommodation contract comparison*

	Rights	Responsibilities
OPTION 1		
Before moving		
While living		
On leaving		

You will need a table for each option you are considering, and quite a bit more space, so draw your own columns on any piece of paper, or download a smart PDF to print or type into from www.downsizingmadesimple.com.au.

Crunching the numbers

While the purchase price of your new home may be obvious, there can be a lot more to the transaction than that.

Even if your new home is a familiar freehold or strata-title, you will need to factor in stamp duty, any ongoing owners corporation fees, and the potential for maintenance costs or special levies. In the case of retirement villages and land lease communities, there may be exit fees involving complicated Deferred Management Fee (DMF) calculations. The DMF is typically a percentage of either your purchase price (which you know) or your future sale price (which you would need to estimate). At exit, you may also be sharing in capital gain or loss with the village operator and you may need to pay for renovations, marketing fees and selling costs.

Granny flat arrangements are normally made with family members, but that doesn't mean they are free. You will still need to work out how much you pay upfront, while you live there, and when you leave. In most granny flat arrangements the exit fee is 100%, i.e. you don't get any of the amount you have paid back. In some cases, normally because of state planning laws, you may actually need to pay to have your granny flat removed and the landscaping reinstated after you leave.

Breaking the costs down by timing can really help to see what you are paying, and when. There's the *ingoing* costs, before you move in; the *ongoing* costs that you pay while you live there; and the *outgoing* costs, due when you leave. It also means that you can compare options more easily.

EXERCISE 5: *Ingoing, ongoing, and outgoing costs*

OPTIONS			
Ingoing			
Ongoing			
Outgoing			

You will need a table for each option you are considering, and quite a bit more space, so draw your own columns on any piece of paper, or download a smart PDF to print or type into from www.downsizingmadesimple.com.au.

Moving costs money

Moving house involves time, effort, and stress, as well as money, which means that you don't want to do it more often than is necessary.

Making sure you know your moving costs for downsizing means that you will know how much you will have left over to invest or spend. Many people simply compare the price they are getting for their existing home with the price they are going to pay for their new one, but this is a recipe for disaster because the cost of moving can easily run to tens of thousands.

Breaking down your costs into selling, moving, and buying costs can help you to budget.

Selling costs

The big costs you need to think about when it comes to selling your home usually involve repaying debt, preparing your home for sale, and paying agents fees and costs.

The most obvious cost of repaying the funds you have borrowed is the principal, but if you are on a fixed rate home loan there can also be penalties for paying early. Make sure you ask your bank for a statement in advance, so you don't get a nasty surprise. Then there's fees for a conveyancer or solicitor to arrange for the contract of sale and lodging of other documents to enable the transfer of ownership. Conveyancing costs range between $500 and $2,500 at time of writing, depending on who you use and how complex the transaction is. On top of the conveyancing costs there will be disbursements, such as fees for settlement, certificates, and a range of searches, including council and water rates, roads, land tax, and heritage listings. You should allow at least $250 for disbursements.

Making your home "sale ready" can cost you too: from big ticket items like renovations, staging furniture if you have already moved out or just need some extra pieces to create a more modern look, and possibly storage costs for furniture and items that you don't want to display while you are selling the home.

There are fees for your real estate agent too. These typically include marketing fees to list your property on websites and in magazines and newspapers, and the agent's sales commission, which is normally 2–3% of the final sale price. If your home is going to be sold by auction, you should expect to pay an auctioneer's fee too: between $500 and $1,000 is common.

Your home will need a thorough clean after you move, something you probably won't have the time or energy to tackle. Booking a cleaning company to do a deep clean will normally cost $500–$1000, depending on how many rooms you have and whether carpet steam-cleaning is also needed.

Moving costs

Packing all your things ready for the move will cost money. If you do it yourself, it may be as little as a few hundred dollars for packing materials and half a day's truck hire, but few people have the energy to do all of that themselves. If you pack everything yourself and get removalists to load your boxes and furniture into a truck, drive over and drop it off at your new home, the cost will depend on how many boxes and furniture needs to be moved and how far it is going. You can get white glove movers, who will do everything for you: they come in and pack everything, move it to your new home and unpack it all for you. It's a wonderful service, and you pay a premium price for it — although some would argue it is well worth it. If you are looking at using this type of service, you should expect to pay $5,000–$10,000 for a local move and more if it is further away.

In a perfect world, we would all move out of one home and into the next on the same day, but it doesn't always work out like that. So your moving expenses may include rent or short term accommodation costs for the period between moving out and moving in. Of course a cheaper alternative can be to stay with family or friends, but remember that visitors are like milk: they go off after about a week.

Buying costs

The purchase price of your new home is the biggest and most obvious buying cost for you new home, but the other costs — such as stamp duty, more conveyancing costs and transfer fees — can be substantial. Another thing you will probably need to think about is the cost of new furniture and appliances: many people who downsize find that their old furniture doesn't fit or suit their new home, or they simply want to make a fresh start and keep only sentimental pieces, but get new beds, couches, tables and chairs — an exercise that can quickly add up to a major expense.

Exercise 6 steps you through estimating your sale proceeds, buying costs, and moving costs to work out how much you will have left to invest or spend (or both).

EXERCISE 6: *Adding up your total moving costs*

Selling		
Expected/Agreed sale value of current home	Fill in all light-coloured fields that apply to your situation, then calculate subtotals.	
Less any debt		
Net sale value		*A*
Renovations (if any)		
Marketing fees		
Agent's commission		
Auctioneer's fee		
Conveyancing		
Storage		
Staging		
Cleaning		
Subtotal of selling costs	*B*	
Total sale proceeds	*A – B = C*	*C*

Buying		
Expected/Agreed purchase price of new home		D
Stamp duty		
Conveyancing		
Transfer fees		
New furniture, appliances		
Subtotal of buying costs	E	
Total buying costs	D + E = F	F
Moving costs		
Removalist fees		
Transferring utilities		
Rent/Temporary accommodation		
Total moving costs	G	
Funds remaining to invest or spend	C – (F + G) = H	H

If you'd rather have the calculations done for you, use the calculator provided at www.downsizingmadesimple.com.au.

Try before you buy

When did you last live with your children? If you are thinking of moving in with one of them — and their partner —
perhaps you should give it a whirl before you commit. The
family dynamics will be completely different, particularly
as you are no longer the head of the household, and everyone needs to make adjustments. Even though the granny
flat space may not yet exist, it's wise to give yourselves
an experimental time of sharing your day-to-day lives —
more than family holidays, house or pet sitting, or Sunday
dinners.

Similarly, if your next move is to a new community —
whether that's the result of a tree change, sea change or a
move to a retirement community — then it may be wise to
rent for a period of time before you commit to buying. The
place where you have always enjoyed your Christmas holidays may not be the place you want to live in the middle
of winter, when there aren't as many people around and
the weather isn't very good. Some people say that "rent
money is dead money," but if you rent for 6 or 12 months
and realise that it really isn't for you, the cost is likely to be
a fraction of what it would have been if you had sold your
home, moved, and then moved again.

If you're trying to find the right retirement community,
the biggest dictator of your ability to enjoy the village is
probably going to be something you can't see or touch —
to quote that great Australian movie *The Castle:* "It's the
vibe". The vibe of the community can be hard to gauge
from guided tours and brochures, because it comes from
the daily interaction with other residents, their interests,
life experiences and topics of conversation. Many retire-

ment communities have open days and social functions that people considering moving to the village can attend. Do it — as this will be the best test for whether you will enjoy living in the village.

Some retirement communities let people "try before they buy". If this option is available, seriously consider moving in for a short stay (the time frames on these offers vary from a weekend to a 12-month lease) with a view to buying in if you are happy. If you are moving a significant distance from where you currently live — for example, escaping the cold southern states for the blue skies and sunshine of Queensland — make sure you experience the "off season" (the peak of Queensland's summer), so you are sure you will really enjoy living in the new location.

Retirement communities

Determining whether you can afford to live in your preferred retirement community is about much more than comparing the amount of money you will get from selling your home with the amount you are going to pay for your new home. The type of retirement community you select will affect whether you are considered a homeowner or non-homeowner for pension purposes and whether or not you will be eligible for rent assistance. If you live in a land lease community and receive a pension, you may be eligible to receive rent assistance (an added bonus) to help meet the ongoing fees. If you live in a retirement village, then you can qualify for rent assistance if you pay an amount equal to or less than $242,000 for your home. In either case the amount of rent assistance you will receive is based on the ongoing costs of living in the community.

Your ongoing costs really have two components: your cost of living (food, utilities, clothing, car maintenance, as well as big ticket items like travel) and the costs associated with living in your home and community. Doing a budget that accounts for all expenses is a good idea.

While you may not be concerned today about what you will get back (and how soon) when you leave the village, it is worth giving some thought to. If you need to estimate a sale price in order to calculate your exit entitlement, our tip is to be conservative. Once you have an idea of your exit entitlement, think about whether that amount of money is likely to mean that you can afford another move, should that be necessary.

2

SELLING YOUR HOME

Leaving a home full of memories can be an emotional experience. It helps to offset the sadness with the excitement of your new home and the prospect of happy times to come. In this chapter, we will show you how to make the sales process as easy as possible.

Should you sell before you buy or buy before you sell?

It's a common real estate conundrum: should you sell your current home before you buy your new one, or the other way around? As with so many things, there's no right or wrong answer, and there are quite a few things to consider. Let's look at both options.

Selling first is generally viewed as the more conservative option, so let's start with that. By selling before you buy elsewhere, you have the advantage of knowing how much your home has sold for and when you can expect your funds (the settlement date). With this information you can "shop to a price" based on the amount of money you want to have left over to spend or invest. There are two key risks. The first is that you can't find anything you want to buy on the market at that time — after all, most settlement periods are 90 days or less. So you may need to move twice: once to a temporary home while you keep looking, and then on to your next home. Sometimes the interim home can be with family or friends, or it may be a rental in the area that you wish to buy in (in which case you may need to take a lease of 6 or 12 months). The second risk of this strategy is market risk: if properties go up in value while you are looking, because you have already sold you are not receiving those gains, and yet the price of your new home is going up. Of course, the reverse can happen too, which is a much better outcome: you can sell and while you are looking for your new home prices drop, increasing your buying power.

If you buy first, you have the advantage of knowing where you are going. In an ideal world, you then put your home on the market, find a buyer at the price you expect fairly quickly, and can make the settlement of both homes on the same day, so that you receive the money for your home and use that to pay for your new one. There are some pretty obvious risks associated with this strategy: no-one may want to buy your property when you wish to sell, or buyers may not be willing to pay the price you want.

There are some things you can do to mitigate these risks, however. One is to make the purchase of your new home subject to the sale of your current home. It is a relatively common term in real estate contracts, because very few people can afford to keep their current home and pay for a new home. If you are buying into a retirement village or land lease community you will generally find that they are quite flexible around such a term, but if your new home is freehold or strata — particularly if it is being sold at auction — you may find that they say no.

If the timing of the sale of your old home and the purchase of your new home don't marry up, you may need to borrow to bridge the gap. Similarly, if you want to buy a home that is more expensive than you sold for and don't want to — or can't — use other funds to pay the difference, you may need to borrow. See *Chapter 5*.

Find the right agent

A good agent doesn't just sell your house. They also help you identify any improvements that may be worth making, suggest how best to present your home to appeal to a wide range of buyers, and put you in contact with service providers who can help. So start looking for your agent early.

You may already know an agent, or have a friend or neighbour who does. But is he or she the right agent to sell your house? While many people just go to the agent they know (or know of) it can pay to shop around. It is definitely worth talking to more than one agent. A good starting point is to drive around your area and see which agents have the most signs. They are the ones who will be most active in your area. Another great resource is *realestate. com.au*, which will show you, not only who's selling what, but what properties are in competition with yours, and at what prices.

If you have a wide choice, identify several agents who have successfully sold properties similar to yours in the area. Ask for their recommendations for getting your home market-ready, an estimated sale price, marketing strategy and method of sale: auction, private sale or sale by set date … While this will leave you with a swag of information to decipher, it gives you a good chance to weigh up different approaches before you work out which one to go with.

If that all sounds too hard, there are web-based services like Agent Select and Local Agent Finder that can help you to select and compare the agents in your area — they will normally give you a report showing the estimated value of your property together with comparable sales in your area. Some will even get the agents to provide you with a breakdown of fees before you meet them, and notify the agents that you've spoken to but didn't choose.

Once you have a sales agent, agree on the final details of the marketing and pricing strategy and work with your agent to prepare the property for sale … then set aside time for the phone calls every week to see how you are going.

Get the best price

How you present your property can have a major influence on how quickly it sells, and the price you get for it.

Should you spend money improving your home to get it ready for sale? It depends! Only spend on things that you — and your agent — are confident will bring a higher price. In most cases, major renovations such as kitchens and bathrooms are best left to the new purchaser, who can create exactly what they want, and "put their stamp" on the property. You should usually focus on fixing the many little things, like broken window-catches, and doors that stick, that can make your property seem unloved. Giving the property a good wash, inside and out, or a new paint job, is often worthwhile too.

If you are going to undertake major renovations, avoid following the latest trends, as these date quickly and are not to everyone's taste. Simple, classic and neutral will appeal to the largest number of buyers. It may be cheaper and easier to have that green bath and matching basin painted white than to renovate the entire bathroom.

While many people see TV shows like "The Block" and think they can renovate their kitchen or bathroom themselves (in a week), it is not as easy as it looks. What's more, it will make you an "owner builder" and you may need to factor in the costs of insurance for your work for up to seven years, and of building reports to satisfy potential buyers that the work is up to standard. Unless you are very experienced, it may also cost you more for a lower quality job. We think it's best to use qualified tradespeople.

Presentation

Presenting your home for sale doesn't need to involve spending a lot of money, but it does take time, planning and effort. A general clean and tidy of house, gardens and grounds is essential. Outside jobs that increase the street appeal are very important: you want your house to give a good impression from the start. Tending to the garden can give a big return on investment — if you have enough time, put in some plants that are due to flower when the property will be on the market. You should also think about pruning trees, cleaning gutters, pressure cleaning paths and fences, and washing or even painting the house.

Show it, stow it or throw it

Inside, you can store — or start packing — things you don't often need: Christmas decorations, books, and all your out-of-season clothes … A cluttered house feels smaller to prospective buyers and gives the impression that there isn't enough storage space.

Paring back decorations and knick-knacks can help buyers see how they can make your place theirs. So keep personal things to a minimum. A huge array of family photos that completely cover your mantlepiece or line an entire wall may be best packed up ready for your move during the sale process. It will make the house feel bigger and help prospective buyers imagine themselves in the house. Listen to your agent's advice: some things that hold a special place in your heart may not be your prospective buyers' taste.

If you are moving to your new house before you sell the old one, hiring furniture or getting a property stylist may be a good idea. Most people find it easier to picture themselves living in a house when they see it furnished.

De-cluttering

This is the perfect time to de-clutter. As you downsize, you are making choices about how your life will change. You'll be letting go of some things, and embracing others. We will outline three different de-cluttering techniques, depending on how drastic you need to be.

If I could only take one load, I'd take …

Sit down in your favourite spot in the house, and list the things that you cannot live without. The things you would take with you if you had to pack everything into a single bag/car/truck (depending on the size of your new home) … If it makes it easier, think about it room by room. The trick here is not to leave your seat while you make your list: if you have to go searching for things to keep, they are probably not that important. Once you know what you *really* want, it should be easier to let go of the other things.

This is a terrific method if you are moving from a large space to a much, much smaller one.

Konmari method

Marie Kondo took the world by storm with her Konmari method. Her basic idea is to keep only the things in your life that "spark joy". She suggests that you consider every single item you own, working through them in five categories. You start with your clothes, as most people find it easy to feel whether each item of clothing brings them joy, or has less pleasant associations. Anything that does not spark joy can be thanked and let go from your life. Then you move through books, papers, konomo (which means everything else) and finish with the hardest group: sentimental items. Her method also has a range of simple strategies for storing items so that when you open a drawer or cupboard you can see everything at a glance.

This is an excellent method if you enjoy being methodical, feel burdened by possessions, or want to keep your new place more organised than your current one. There are many books and online resources devoted to the Konmari method.

When did I use it last? and How many do I need?

A completely different approach is to sort through your possessions, discarding anything you haven't used in the past six months (12 months if many things get only seasonal use). When you find multiple items, consider how many you actually need, and keep only that many. For example, if you have six whisks in the kitchen you will probably only keep one or two, but you will probably want more than one or two pairs of socks.

With this method, you start with a room where things are less sentimental, perhaps the kitchen. Getting rid of wooden spoons, mixing bowls and tea towels doesn't tend to get us too misty-eyed and can give you the momentum to tackle the harder stuff — like wardrobes.

This is a handy method for those who don't need to make massive reductions in their belongings. It offers a straightforward framework for deciding what to keep and what is surplus to requirement.

Throw it

This is a great time to cash in old for new. Selling things you don't need any more through a garage sale, local market, or online through sites such as eBay, FaceBook or Gumtree, gives them a new lease of life, and gives you money to pay for your move or buy things that suit your new home. Alternatively you may prefer to "free-cycle" or donate your unwanted things. Many charities will happily come to collect clothing, furniture, sporting equipment and other household items as long as they are in good condition.

Time to move

When it is time to move there is the obvious need to pack up all of your belongings and move to your new home — an arduous but exciting task. Then there are the other, less exciting jobs like arranging removalists, forwarding mail, disconnecting and re-connecting utilities, streaming and internet services and — if you haven't already done it — a top-to-toe clean to get the house ready for its new owners. There are a range of different companies that can assist with these tasks, including at least one (Connect Now) that can do it all, or just the bits you don't want to do.

Planning ahead will make moving much lest stressful, and our moving checklist (*Exercise 7*) will help.

EXERCISE 7: Moving checklist

Before you move

☐ **Reality check:** Get or sketch a floor plan of your new home. Ideally, measure your furniture to make sure everything you want to take is going to fit. Photos of your new place can help you visualise how suited your pieces are to your new home.

☐ **Book a removalist:** It's best to do this as soon as you have a date to move.

☐ **Make as many meals as you can** from the ingredients you have in your pantry, fridge and freezer so there is less food to move and you are not stressed trying to keep things cold.

☐ **Packing:** decide whether to pack and unpack yourself, or employ a packing service. If you want your belongings to be insured during the move, you may need to use professional packers.

If you are packing yourself, read on:

○ Start gathering boxes: Bunnings, your local supermarket or fruit and vegetable shop are all likely to have boxes you can have free of charge. Alternatively, you can buy boxes from your removalist or secondhand from people who have recently moved (through websites like eBay, Facebook or Gumtree).

○ Pack heavy things like books, plates and casserole dishes in small boxes, lighter ones like quilts, pillows and cushions in larger cartons — or use light and soft items to protect fragile items.

○ Label boxes with their contents, or the room they will go into. Mark fragile items in colour to stand out. Write on at least two sides of each box so you can identify what's in them when they are stacked.

Before you move

- O Your most valuable possessions should travel with you. They are often best packed in suitcases, which are more likely to fit easily into a car.
- O Dismantle any furniture that comes apart and keep screws, bolts and allen keys in a safe place (a small box specially for these things with the relevant parts in labelled, individual sandwich bags) or secured to the furniture itself. This can save a lot of time and frustration later.

☐ **Services:**
- O **Arrange disconnections from your old home:** phone, internet, TV, gas, electricity … Remember to leave the power on for a few days if someone will be coming back to clean.
- O **Shop around for new connections at your new home:** phone, internet, TV, gas, electricity …

☐ **Change of address:** Advise Australia Post and other providers of your new address.

☐ **Pack a moving "survival kit":** Pack everything you'll need in your first day or two at the new home: toiletries, medications, scissors, toilet paper and tools, pet requirements, snacks, kettle, tea and coffee, toaster. The last thing you need after a big day moving is to be rummaging through boxes to make a cup of tea or find your much-needed medication.

Before you move

☐ Check the arrangements for your arrival:

    ○ **Timing:** Are there restrictions on times you can move in and monopolise the lifts? Do you need to book in your moving time with a building manager?

    ○ **Keys:** If you don't yet have them, when and where can you collect them? Do you need something extra, such as a swipe card or code for security gates, garage or goods lift?

    ○ **Contacts:** Do you — or your removalists — need to contact anyone in advance, or on arrival, e.g. a site manager?

    ○ **Paperwork:** Is there anything that must be finished before your move, or done on the day, e.g. condition report?

    ○ **Fees:** Do you have to pay anything on moving day?

Moving day

Remember, it is always a big day. By the end of it, you'll probably just be wanting a toasted sandwich or takeaway and an early night!

On moving day, you have a foot in each world. You haven't quite left the old house and you're not in the new one either. But you're responsible for both.

New home

☐ **Access:** Make sure access is clear for your removalists and helpers.

☐ **Utilities:** Check everything that should be connected is connected and working.

New home

☐ **Condition:** Check that the home is as you expected. Complete a condition report, if required, and take photos for your own records.

☐ **Make your bed:** Re-assemble the bed, and get the mattress, with sheets and covers on as your first priority. You are really going to need it later!

☐ **Unpack:** Explain where you want your belongings placed — have boxes clearly marked and help direct the unloading. Make sure your "survival kit" stays accessible. Resist temptation to begin unpacking until it's all brought in.

☐ **Let it settle:** Leave your fridge standing upright for at least three hours before you switch it on, so that the coolant gas can settle after transportation.

☐ **Focus on key areas:** For some people that's the kitchen, for others, the bathroom or the office. Whatever you need most, focus on getting those areas functional for the first couple of days.

Old home

☐ **Check:** Make sure nothing has been left behind.

☐ **Check again:** Arrange any final cleaning.

*If you need to add items, write your own list or download a smart PDF to print or type into from **www.downsizingmadesimple.com.au**.*

Selling your home is often an emotional time, but you can take a lot of the stress out of it by planning ahead.

3

SUPERANNUATION AND THE DOWNSIZING INCENTIVE

What has superannuation got to do with downsizing? Well, it will probably play a big part in the financial strategies you decide to use, so we will remind you of the basics — and a few things relevant to downsizing — in this chapter. The idea of superannuation is simple: you give up a relatively small amount of money throughout your working life, and the power of compounding gives you a larger amount of money to live on when you have stopped working.

Superannuation is a government-sponsored form of compulsory savings: a percentage of your salary is set aside every pay cycle, often pooled with other people's super, and invested in a range of assets.

Super has a few unique advantages:

1. If you wish, the contributions can come out of your pay before you see it, making saving almost painless.
2. Your money is pooled to access a wide range of investments, but it is tracked individually.
3. The government offers fantastic tax breaks for super: low input taxes; a low tax environment while the assets

are growing; and tax-free earnings and pension when you retire.

Putting money in

Because superannuation enjoys valuable tax concessions, there are restrictions on who can make contributions, and on the amounts that can be contributed.

Anybody under the age of 67 can contribute to superannuation, working or not.

Once you reach 67, to make a *concessional* (tax-deductible) contribution you have to satisfy the "work test". This requires you to work for at least 40 hours over 30 consecutive days in the financial year you make the contribution. For example, if you are aged 71 you could work 10 hours a week for four consecutive weeks, or 20 hours a week twice in a month, or 40 hours in one week.

From 1 July 2022 the rules were changed to allow *non-concessional* contributions and *salary-sacrificed concessional contributions* to be made up to age 75, with no need to pass the work test.

Once you reach age 75 you are not allowed to contribute to superannuation, though employers may still make contributions on your behalf.

A person of any age (even 100) may contribute to superannuation on behalf of their spouse provided the spouse is aged less than 67. Neither the spouse nor the contributor has to be working.

You can leave your money in accumulation mode as long as you wish, however, when you move to pension phase minimum annual drawdowns are required.

TABLE 2: *Minimum superannuation drawdowns in pension mode*

Age	Required minimum drawdown	
To 64	4% of balance	at the end of the previous financial year i.e. the minimum drawdown for the 2024 financial year is based on the balance at 30 June 2023
65–74	5% of balance	
75–84	6% of balance	
85–94	10% of balance	
95+	14% of balance	

Types of contributions

There are two types of contributions — those for which somebody claims a tax deduction, and those for which nobody claims a tax deduction. They are treated differently under superannuation regulations so make sure you clearly understand which is which. We will be referring to these two types continually from now on.

- **Concessional contributions** (formerly known as deductible contributions) are made from before-tax dollars. They pay a once-only "contributions tax" of 15% when paid into the fund (30% for high income earners — defined as people with an adjusted taxable income over $250,000). Concessional contributions, including those made by employers, are capped. Since 1 July 2021 the cap has been $27,500 a year for everybody, irrespective of age.

- **Non-concessional contributions** (formerly known as "undeducted contributions") are made from after-tax dollars. There is no contributions tax when these are paid into the fund. From 1 July 2021, each person is limited to $110,000 of these contributions in any year, but a person aged less than 75 can bring forward three years' contributions and contribute $330,000 in one financial year. Of course, having done that, they cannot make any further non-concessional contributions for the next three years. No non-concessional contributions are allowed if your super balance exceeds $1.9 million on 30 June in the year prior to the current one. Also, if your balance is between $1.7 and $1.9 million, the amount you can bring forward is prorated.

The downsizer contribution

In 2018, a new "downsizer contribution" was created, with two aims: to make established homes available in the housing market, and to further support people to fund their own retirement. It enables anybody aged 55 or older who chooses to downsize, to contribute up to $300,000 into superannuation, irrespective of their existing super-annuation balance, and without having to pass the work test. It is, of course, subject to some conditions.

- **Age:** You must be 55 years old or older when you make a downsizer contribution. There is no maximum age limit, and your age at the contract date is not relevant.

- **Asset:** The contribution must come from the proceeds of selling the family home — which must be in Australia, and not be a caravan, houseboat, or other mobile home.

- **Timing:** The contribution must be made within 90 days of receiving the proceeds of the sale. (It is usually made at settlement.) It is possible to apply for an extension in certain circumstances, which should be done within the 90-day period.

- **Ownership:** The home must have been owned by you, your spouse, or former spouse for at least 10 years prior to the contribution being made. This allows some flexibility: the home may have been held solely, jointly or as tenants in common; your spouse may have died during the 10-year period; and, as long as you have had the home for the required 10 year period, it doesn't matter if your spouse is rather newer.

- **Main residence:** The proceeds from the sale of the home must be exempt (or partially exempt) from capital gains tax (CGT) under the main residence exemption. (Partial exemption may be relevant if you used part of your home for running a business.) Remember that you can be away from your main residence for up to six years without losing the CGT exemption, so you can rent your home out and go travelling if that's on your bucket list.

- **Limits:** The downsizer contribution is capped at the lesser of the amount of the sale or $300,000 per person. For example, a couple who sell the family home for $1 million can contribute a maximum of $300,000 each if they meet all the requirements. But if another couple sell their home for $500,000, the maximum they can contribute is $500,000 combined.

- **Eligibility to receive the payment:** If you have a self-managed super fund (SMSF), it may be necessary to amend the trust deed to make the fund eligible to receive the contribution. If you are with an industry or retail fund, you should also check that they are able to receive the downsizer contribution, as it could be disastrous for your plans if they cannot.

  The downsizer contribution can be made irrespective of your total superannuation balance. The limit on non-concessional contributions does not apply.

- **Tax and superannuation status:**
  - The downsizer contribution is included in the tax-free component of your fund, so it cannot be claimed as a tax deduction.
  - The $1.9 million limit on the amount that can be transferred into super in pension mode (your *transfer balance cap*) will still apply. This means that if you have already used up all or part of your transfer balance cap, all or part of the downsizer contribution would have to be held in accumulation mode, where you'll need to plan for the earnings being taxed a flat 15% from the first dollar earned.

- **Once-only strategy:** You only have one chance to make a downsizer contribution (though it may be paid in multiple transactions). Even if you do not have the resources to contribute $300,000 each from the sale of the family home, the unused amount cannot be carried forward.

Is it right for you?

Even a couple aged 85 with $2 million each in superannuation would be eligible to make the downsizer contribution. But is it a good idea? It is important to take advice about the best strategy for *you* to use, if you are considering making a downsizer contribution.

While it is exempt from the total superannuation balance test, it *does* add to your total superannuation balance. For example, if you had $1.7 million in superannuation, then made a downsizer contribution of $300,000, your superannuation balance would be over the $1.9 million limit and you could not make any more non-concessional contributions.

If you receive any age pension, investigate the Centrelink implications. When you downsize you are normally moving to a house of less value than the one you currently occupy, so you are turning part of an exempt asset — the family home — into an assessable asset such as superannuation, shares or interest-bearing accounts. Because of the way the assets test works, you could lose up to $7,800 a year for each $100,000 converted.

CASE STUDY — Ron and Sara

Ron and Sara, both aged 75, have a house worth $1,200,000, $400,000 in superannuation, $50,000 in personal effects such as furniture and motor vehicles, and receive the full age pension. Their house is getting too big, so they are contemplating downsizing to a property worth around $700,000. This would free up around $400,000 after costs of relocating.

That money may be of little benefit to them. Once you reach pensionable age all financial assets are assessable, whether they are held inside or outside superannuation. They would be converting part of a non-assessable asset, the family home, into an assessable asset, cash. Their total assessable assets would rise by $400,000 to $800,000 and their pension would fall by $31,100 a year.

Ron and Sara would have to work out if the increase in income from the extra $400,000 invested would compensate for the loss of over $31,000 a year in pension. If they achieved a return of 5% per year on the new investments, they would still have close to a $11,000 annual shortfall. Another factor to consider is what further capital gain their home might make if they delayed moving for a few more years while the capital in their super ran down. They may well take the view that the combination of the capital gain and maintaining the full pension would outweigh the advantages of moving.

Of course there are exceptions. Gus and Constance, aged 76 and 78, want to withdraw money from their superannuation to buy a house to downsize into, before they sell the family home. They want to re-contribute the money to super when the sale proceeds of the family home are to

> *hand. Under the previous rules they could not do this, as they have passed the age limit for contributions and also are retired — under the new rules, they can contribute up to $600,000.*

The downsizer contribution strategy can be useful in certain cases, but get expert advice and do the numbers on any proposed change of residence. It will cost tens of thousands of dollars to change properties, and loss of pension could cost a couple up to $43,000 per year. You would have to be a lot better off for making the contribution.

Also, given that a couple can have $800,000 in investments outside superannuation and pay no income tax, thanks to the tax-free threshold and various offsets, it may be better to hold money in personal names.

Growing your money in super

When you make regular contributions to superannuation, you are practising the proven investment strategy of dollar-cost averaging, which helps smooth out market volatility.

Choosing the right investment mix

Rate of return is one of the key elements affecting how long your superannuation lasts. Unfortunately, many people rarely think about their super, and when they do, they allow fear of losing money to dominate and make an overly conservative investment choice that offers a relatively low rate of return.

The best option is to have a relationship with a good financial adviser, and once a year review your whole portfolio to ensure it is appropriate for your goals and your risk profile. There is no reason to rush to the perceived security of a capital stable option if you are in accumulation mode and making regular contributions. Once you approach retirement, you should make sure you have around 2 to 3 years' planned expenditure in a cash-based option, part of your money in capital stable, and the rest in growth. Keep in mind that if you retire at 65, you may have 30 years ahead of you — you don't want to run the risk of lasting longer than your money.

Tax breaks on fund earnings

When superannuation funds are in accumulation mode, they pay a flat tax rate of 15% a year on earnings, which makes them an efficient vehicle for holding income-earning assets. Costs of running the fund and insurance premiums are allowable deductions, and imputation credits on shares plus depreciation allowances on property-based investments can reduce or eliminate the tax altogether.

Pension funds are tax-free funds and the account-based pension itself is tax-free for all those aged 60 and over.

How much can you have in super?

There is currently no limit as to how much you can hold in superannuation, though there is a limit to the amount you can have in a tax-free pension fund. This limit was first applied from 1 July 2017: a limit of $1.6 million was placed on the amount that can be transferred to the tax-free pension. Thanks to indexation, this has risen to $1,900,000 from 1 July 2023. Once you have maxed out the amount you can transfer to your superannuation pension mode, the money is free to grow to any sum, provided you keep taking out the minimum pension. Just bear in mind that if you have money in both pension mode and accumulation mode, and you wish to take a lump-sum payment, it's best to take it from the accumulation fund.

There is still no limit on the amount that can be held in the concessionally taxed accumulation phase. However, the government has proposed a special surcharge of 30% on individual balances over $3 million from 1 July 2026.

Taking money out

There are basically five types of income sources you can have when you retire:

1. An account-based pension from your superannuation fund
2. An annuity
3. A lifetime income product
4. Income from independent investments
5. The age pension

These income streams are all discussed in great detail in Noel's book, *Retirement Made Simple,* so we are giving only a brief overview here. Just keep in mind that some annuities and lifetime income products now have major Centrelink concessions — as much as 40% of the capital invested in them is exempt from the Centrelink assets test. As a result they are very popular with retirees who are either right at the Centrelink assets cut-off point or just over it. For example, $300,000 invested in one of these products may increase your age pension by $9,360 per year, and you also receive a lifetime income from the product. They are discussed in more detail in the next chapter.

Account-based pensions

An account-based pension is one of the most common income streams used by Australian retirees. You simply draw a pension from your superannuation fund, and provided you take the minimum repayments each year the fund remains tax-free and the income you receive is also tax-free. The big advantage is that your money is always at call, so if you need to withdraw a lump sum for an emergency the money is there. However, to achieve the returns necessary for a long life you need to have at least part of your superannuation in growth-based assets, such as local and overseas shares, which by their nature are volatile, therefore, your capital will most likely rise and fall with the market.

Annuities

You hand the fund manager a lump sum, and in return they promise to pay you an income for a set period, or for life. The advantage is that you have the certainty of a the regular income from the product; the disadvantage is that annuities are inflexible — if you change your mind after a certain period, there are usually heavy exit fees. They need to be tailored to your own circumstances, as they have many options, and in some cases have the Centrelink concessions mentioned previously.

An alternative to receiving an annuity that locks in a fixed rate is an *investment-linked annuity*, where income payments are linked to the value of the investment options chosen. The advantage of these types of annuities is that over your lifetime the income may be greater than what you may have otherwise locked in under a regular lifetime annuity arrangement. Like traditional lifetime annuities, you don't have the flexibility to withdraw from the arrangement, but you can generally change your investment mix as your investment requirements change over time.

Lifetime income streams

This product is growing in popularity, and the number of funds offering them is also increasing. They all carry the Centrelink concession and need to be tailored to your own situation. Like annuities, they offer the certainty of a lifetime income stream, but no lump sum withdrawals can be made, so they lack flexibility.

Living off your investments

This refers to income from property or shares in most cases, and is suitable for people who do not trust superannuation, or who are at an age where they cannot contribute to superannuation. There could be good options for people who like to do their own thing, but you lose the tax concessions that may be available if the money was in superannuation instead. However, you don't have the ongoing fees of super nor the death tax, which may be levied if part of your superannuation is left to a non-dependent.

Stay in super?

Finally, the big question for many people after retirement is whether to keep their assets in superannuation, or cash them in and invest them in their own names. It is not a one-size-fits-all situation, so make sure you think about your own personality and confidence in investing, as well as getting specific financial advice for your situation.

Every case is different, but one thing is certain: the higher the net return you can achieve on your assets the longer your money will last. But stick to good, long term investments and avoid gambling. If you are not sure which is which, consider that any investment whose performance you watch on your phone minute-by-minute is a gamble not an investment. There is also the sleep-at-night factor: if you are not comfortable managing your own money, let full-time professional fund managers do it for you.

CASE STUDY — Jack and Ellen

Jack and Ellen are retired and their sole financial asset (after paying off their home loan) is $400,000 in super. They can leave it in super and move it to pension mode, where the money will be in a tax-free environment. The cost of this approach is ongoing fees, the risk of the rules changing, and the possibility of a death tax of 17% when they die, if they are leaving their money to a non-dependent, such as an adult child.

Or they could cash the money out, and invest the assets in managed funds in their own names. They may well have 30 years to live, so keeping their money in the bank is not appropriate. If they invest in a typical balanced portfolio comprising 20% cash, 40% Australian shares,

30% international shares, and 10% listed property, the income from the portfolio should be around $14,800 per year, plus franking credits of $2,752. The estimated capital growth would be $16,400 per year, but no tax is payable on this until the asset is disposed of, which may be years down the track. Even then, it enjoys a 50% discount, because the asset was held for more than one year.

They are way under the tax-free threshold, so the money is still in a tax-free environment. Furthermore, they should get a bonus from the full refund of the franking credits. And they will still be eligible for a part pension, whether they keep the money inside or outside super. Jack and Ellen are confident that they can select appropriate managed funds, and they decide to take this route.

CASE STUDY — Mariana

Mariana wrote to tell us she was single, aged 70, and on the full age pension. Her major asset was $80,000 in her superannuation fund, which was paying her a monthly income. She wanted to know whether she should stay in superannuation or cash it in.

Our first thought was to cash her super in. That way she could save ongoing fees and be free of the death tax that might be incurred by her beneficiaries when she died.

"But what am I going to do with the money?" she asked. "The banks are paying less than 2%." The fund, after fees, had been paying her between 6% and 8% a year. The only way for her to get better returns would be to invest in a range of managed funds that were heavily invested in the share market.

> *Mariana was obviously inexperienced in do-it-yourself investing, which meant she would need to get advice. The challenge is that the financial advice industry is so heavily regulated that to get advice she would need a full financial analysis, which involves a long consultation and would cost at least $3,000.*
>
> *In the end, Mariana was probably better off to leave her finances be. She could relax and enjoy the monthly income, and the fact that her money was being professionally managed, and still make withdrawals at call whenever she needed money.*

Death and taxes

You can't take it with you, but most people still care what happens to their assets after they die, particularly when they have family or favoured charities to support.

Most Australians believe we don't have death taxes here. They'd be wrong. Superannuation death benefits may be subject to tax of 15% (or 17%, when it includes the Medicare levy). Take the time to get your head around this — it's an easy tax to minimise with a bit of planning.

First, it applies only to the taxable component of your superannuation, which comprises concessional contributions plus accrued fund earnings. Second, it applies only to money that is given to a non-dependent. A spouse is always classed as a dependent, whether they have a separate income or not.

A way to minimise the death tax, if you are eligible both to contribute to superannuation and to make tax-free withdrawals from your superannuation fund, is to withdraw and then re-contribute those contributions as non-concessional contributions. This will not wipe out the entire taxable component, but it will certainly reduce it. Watch the contribution limits, if you choose to do this — there are big penalties for exceeding the caps.

Another way to minimise the death tax, if you know that death is imminent, is to withdraw all or most of your superannuation and do whatever you wish with it. There would be no tax on the withdrawal, and you could put the money into a bank account to be distributed in accordance with the terms of your will after your death.

Of course most of us don't know when we will die. So if you have money you want to leave to non-dependents, it is worth reviewing whether keeping your investments inside super is the best strategy.

A further option to consider is using an investment bond to avoid the death tax — investment bonds are a tax-effective alternative to help build wealth. They can also be used in estate planning to transfer wealth between generations efficiently and tax-effectively. They are particularly useful if you want to ensure that death benefits are passed on to beneficiaries outside of your estate, avoiding challenges to your will.

Unlike superannuation death benefits paid to a non-dependent (where the taxable component will attract tax at a rate of 17%, including the Medicare levy, payable by the beneficiary) death benefit proceeds from an investment bond do not attract any additional tax, whether paid to a dependent or non-dependent.

Benefit payments can be directed to any legal entity, including individuals (whether related to you or not), trusts, and companies. They can even be directed to a charity. All death benefit nominations are binding and not subject to trustee or issuer discretion, so the benefits will reach those you intend to provide for.

In some cases, issuers will provide the option to transfer ownership of an investment bond and provide a regular payment to the nominated beneficiary. Like superannuation, investment bonds can provide for investment choice, so you control what the bond is being invested in. Investment bonds are also a tax-paid structure, again similar to superannuation, however a maximum tax rate of 30% applies. Depending on the provider, the effective long term tax rate on the earnings can be lower. Unlike superannuation, however, there are no limits on how much can be contributed and you don't need to retire to access your money.

CASE STUDY — Mary

Mary, now aged 84, has an allocated pension account and an SMSF account in accumulation phase with a taxable balance of $600,000. Mary would like to provide those funds to her adult daughter, however, under superannuation rules, the benefit payment would be taxed at 17%, including the Medicare levy.

Mary decides to withdraw those funds and invest the proceeds into an investment bond with the same investment strategy. While the investment bond's standard tax rate is higher than her superannuation tax rate, she believes that avoiding the death tax of $102,000 (17% of $600,000) will more than offset this.

When you die, your superannuation is not disbursed in terms of your will — the trustee of your superannuation fund decides which beneficiaries will get your money. This is not necessarily a problem if your affairs are simple, but challenges can arise if there is tension between potential beneficiaries, such as children from multiple relationships. These challenges can be avoided by making a binding death benefit nomination, which requires the trustee of your superannuation fund to act in terms of the document. However, this document should not be executed without good advice, because it means the executor of your estate loses flexibility.

CASE STUDY

A couple went to a seminar where Noel was discussing potential family conflicts and the use of a death benefit nomination. Without taking advice, they promptly executed a binding death benefit nomination leaving half of their superannuation to each other, and the balance to be divided equally between their two children, who were high earning professionals.

The husband died suddenly, leaving $4 million in super-annuation. If there had been no death benefit nomination, the whole $4 million could have been left to the widow tax-free. However, because of the binding nomination, the trustee was obliged to pay $2 million tax-free to the widow, and $1 million to each of the two children. The death tax on that was $170,000 to each child — a total of $340,000.

If you are considering making a binding death benefit nomination, first make sure you clearly understand the implications. A binding nomination can only be made to a dependent (as defined in superannuation law) or legal personal representative (your executor). Once a valid binding nomination is in place, the trustee must follow it, even if your circumstances have changed — so they lose the discretion to distribute the proceeds of your fund in the most tax-effective manner.

4

PENSION PLANNING

This chapter covers the age pension system in a very brief way, focusing on the mechanics of pensions rather than the numbers. This is because the dollar figures for eligibility tests and the pension itself are continually changing. While figures may well be out of date at the time you read this book, pensions will probably still work in the same way.

Relaxation of the age pension assets test in September 2007 meant that many Australians were eligible to receive an age pension for the first time. Of course, on 1 January 2017 they changed again, enabling pensioners to have more assets, but doubling the rate at which pension reduced beyond the thresholds. The rules are a bit like fashion really: up, down and round in cycles.

If you are eligible for a full pension currently you would get:

- $1,097/fortnight if you are single
- $827/fortnight each, if you are a member of a couple. If only one partner is eligible, they are assessed based on the combined assets and income of the couple, but the maximum they can receive is less than receiving the single pension.
- up to $1,654/fortnight together (twice $827), if both members of a couple are eligible for the pension

- up to $2,194/fortnight together (twice the single pension), if both members of a couple are eligible for the pension, and they are separated by illness.

Are you eligible?

First, you have to be of pensionable age, which is now 67. Pension age has been increasing by six months every 2 years since 2015, from 1 July 2023 it is 67. This is currently the final increase to age pension age, although there are discussions about increasing the age to 70.

You also need to meet the residency rules. On the day that you claim the age pension you must be living in Australia, physically in Australia, and an Australian resident. As a general rule you must have been an Australian resident for at least 10 years in total, with at least 5 of those years consecutive (i.e. no break in your residency). There are special exemptions for people who are or were refugees, widows, and people who have lived or worked overseas in certain countries that Centrelink has agreements with.

Assuming you meet the age and residency requirements, the amount of age pension you can get is based on your means. Centrelink uses both an assets and an income test, and applis the one that gives you the *least* pension. Since 20 September 2023, the cut-off point for assets was $1,003,000 for a homeowner couple and $667,500 for a single homeowner.

People who don't own a home, or who live in a granny flat or retirement village and have paid an amount below the entry contribution limit (currently $242,000) can be assessed as a non-homeowner. Non-homeowners have the value of their dwelling included in the assets test, but the assets test threshold applied is $242,000 higher — so it cancels out, and if the value of the dwelling is significantly under the limit, it can even be an advantage. The other advantage to being a non-homeowner is that you are generally able to claim rent assistance on top of your pension.

Under the income test, the pension cut-off points are $95,337 per annum for a couple, with a higher cut-off point of $123,417 for couples separated by illness, and $62,332 for a single. If your income or assets exceed the cut-offs, you lose the pension.

TABLE 3: *Age pension asset and income thresholds and cut-offs, at 20 September 2023*

ASSETS TEST

	Homeowner		Non-homeowner	
	Threshold	Cut-off	Threshold	Cut-off
Single	$301,750	$667,500	$543,750	$909,500
Couple	$451,500	$1,003,000	$693,500	$1,245,000
Couple (separated by illness)	$451,500	$1,183,000	$693,500	$1,425,000

INCOME TEST (PER FORTNIGHT)

	Income threshold	Income cut-off
Single	$204	$2,397.40
Couple	$360	$3,666.80
Couple (separated by illness)	$360	$4,746.80

Rent assistance

Rent assistance is a payment that goes on top of your pension, so if your pension is zero then you can't qualify for rent assistance. If you qualify for the age pension, you don't own your home (or you own your home but don't own the land on which it sits such as in a caravan park or land lease community), and you pay at least the minimum amount of rent, then you can qualify for rent assistance.

Rent assistance is quite a generous payment, calculated at 75 cents for each dollar of rent you pay above the threshold. The threshold for singles is $143 per fortnight and for couples it is $232, there are not many rents that you can find for less than that! With the thresholds so low most people who pay rent, which can include the ongoing costs in a retirement village or site fees in a caravan park or land lease community, are eligible for assistance. Of course you can't pay rent of $1,000 per fortnight and get the government to pay 75% above the threshold, the maximum amount of rent assistance that singles can claim is $185 per fortnight, which you would be eligible for if your rent was $390 per fortnight (or more). For couples, the maximum rent assistance payment is $174 per fortnight, to receive that amount your rent would need to be at least $465 per fortnight. These are the rates and thresholds for singles who live alone and couples who live together. Different rates and thresholds apply to sharers and couples who are separated.

TABLE 4: *Rent assistance thresholds and payments,*
at 20 September 2023

Rent assistance fortnightly	Rent threshold	Maximum payment	Rent to receive maximum payment
Single	$143.40	$184.80	$389.80
Couple	$232.40	$174.00	$464.40

Assets

Everything you own — including your superannuation — is an asset, with two exceptions. The big one is your home, if you own one. Funeral bonds to a value of $15,000 are also excluded from both the assets test and the income test. We will explain more about these later. Your chattels (such as furniture, car and boat) are valued at second-hand sale value, not replacement value. This puts a top figure of $5,000 on most people's furniture. Thus, a couple could live in a multi-million-dollar home, earn $90,000 a year, have assets worth $900,000, and still get a small part age pension and all the goodies that go with it.

Assets test strategies

While the age pension asset threshold (under which you receive the full pension) and cut-off point (over which you receive nothing) are reasonably liberal, the rate at which your pension reduces between these two figures is quite harsh. It is called the taper rate and under the assets test it is currently $3 per thousand dollars of assets above the threshold per fortnight. When expressed like that it doesn't sound so punitive, but in essence it is a negative

7.8% return, because for each $100,000 your assets exceed the threshold your pension reduces by $7,800 per year, regardless of whether you are single or a couple. That amount of income is difficult to replace: impossible if you are trying to do so without volatile assets such as shares and property.

So sometimes it is worth reducing your assessable assets. You can give some of your money away, but get advice first. Centrelink limits what you can give, currently to $10,000 in a financial year with a maximum of $30,000 over five financial years. Using these rules, a would-be pensioner could give away $10,000 before June 30 and $10,000 just after it to quickly reduce their assessable assets by $20,000.

Pensioners may also reduce assessable assets by spending money on their own home, on living expenses and travelling, or by selling the home they have and buying a more expensive one to live in. These methods will all use up surplus assessable assets, but should only be done after a lot of thought. There is no point in doing foolish things just for the sake of the pension.

Many people's financial plan in downsizing is to free up some of the capital tied up in the family home, either to invest for income, or to buy some lifestyle assets, like a new car, caravan or boat. But if you receive a pension you need to make sure you crunch the numbers on this strategy: examine the impact to your pension under both the asset and income tests. If you are purchasing lifestyle assets, they don't produce income, nor are they deemed to earn income for pension purposes — they are simply assets. If you are buying off the showroom floor remember that the moment you drive away that car, boat or caravan it has lost value — and the value you need to declare and be assessed on is the price you would get if you turned around and sold it now, *not* what you have just paid for it.

Others intend to supersize their downsize — they are paying more for their new home than they get for their old one. It is common to see this when people are moving closer to town, or to a whole new area, where the property prices are quite different from their current area. If you receive a pension you need to crunch the numbers on this strategy too. Such a move *may* increase your pension entitlement. Of course you can never get more than the maximum entitlement so there is a point beyond which you have gone too far, but if you are currently a part pensioner this move may see you get more pension or potentially the full amount.

Funeral bonds

Funeral bonds are friendly society bonds that enjoy a low tax status. Earnings compound on the money invested until your death. Neither the accruing returns nor the value of the bond are assessed under income or assets tests unless you invest more than the allowed amount. Pensioners in a couple may invest up to $15,000 each in a maximum of two funeral bonds and the balance will not be assessed for the income or assets test. Don't be tempted by a "joint" funeral bond: it is still limited to $15,000, and can only be drawn on when the second person dies. Funeral bonds can be useful for reducing assets and income by a small amount. Keep in mind that the money cannot be withdrawn until death — but any funds surplus to funeral costs will be refunded to the estate.

We have found that many pensioners feel comfortable putting $5,000–$10,000 in funeral bonds, so they know there will be money for a simple funeral.

If you want something more elaborate, a funeral bond may not be the best investment: the money simply won't be enough to meet the cost. If you know what you want — or perhaps you just want more control over your funeral — then a prepaid funeral may be the choice for you. Just remember it's one or the other: a funeral bond or a prepaid funeral, and in either case you may also purchase a burial plot.

There is no limit to the amount that you can spend on a plot or a prepaid funeral, and given the relatively low returns on funeral bonds compared with inflation on funeral costs it may be a good investment. But unlike a funeral bond, a prepaid funeral locks in specific arrangements with a specific provider. If you later want to transfer these benefits it is not simple and may be expensive. And of course, you will have to make sure your family are fully aware of what you have arranged.

Estate planning

Pensioners should be careful when making wills, as the amount of allowable assets for a single person is less than that for a couple.

> **CASE STUDY — Harry and Mabel**
>
> *Harry and Mabel had assessable assets of $700,000 and were getting a part pension. Harry died suddenly and left all his assets to Mabel. This took her over the assets test limit, and she lost the pension entirely. She gifted some of the money to her kids and in five years time she will get her pension back. Had Harry left the money to the kids as part of the estate, she would have been able to maintain her pension — plus all the associated benefits.*

If pensioners have nobody to leave their money to, they could consider leaving it to some of the many worthwhile charities that exist. They are usually run by hard-working volunteers who can get a great deal of value out of a little extra money. This is far better than leaving it to people you have never met or letting it end up in general revenue.

Income

The income test is a simple one: your financial assets are assessed on a notional rate of return called the "deeming rate", which is adjusted in line with prevailing investment returns — although unlike the consumer price index (CPI) where the "basket of goods" is known, the investment mix the government use for the deeming rates is not disclosed. Where they are actually invested, and what they are actually earning, is not relevant — only the deeming rate is. Currently, your financial assets are deemed to be earning 0.25% for the first $100,200 ($60,400 for singles), and 2.25% on the balance. For example, if a couple had $300,000 of financial assets, their deemed income would be $4,746/year. That is, 0.25% on $100,200 ($250.50) plus 2.25% on $199,800 ($4,495.50).

"Financial assets" include bank accounts, debentures, shares, managed funds, and friendly society and insurance bonds. If you have an account-based pension, it is subject to the deeming rules unless you commenced the pension before 1 January 2015 *and* on 31 December 2014 you held a Commonwealth Seniors Health Card and you continue to hold it. If these criteria are met, the assessment of your pension will be grandfathered.

If your deemed assets are below the lower amount, you can probably calculate it in your head. Above the lower assets amount you can use *Exercise 8* to quickly calculate your deemed income.

EXERCISE 8: *Deemed income calculator*

	Asset threshold	Rate	Deemed income	Your total
Lower rate	Single $60,400	0.25%	$151/year	*Transfer the appropriate figure from left.*
	Couple $100,200	0.25%	$250.50/ year	$_____ / year
Upper rate	Assets over your threshold $_____	2.25%	$_____ / year Calculate (Assets x 2.25%)	$_____ / year *Add figure above and figure at left to see your total income.*

If you'd rather have the calculations done for you, use the calculator provided at www.downsizingmadesimple.com.au.

Property other than your home

If you have an investment property, holiday home or even vacant land, it is not subject to deeming, the actual income is assessed. This is based on the income (rent) minus deductions (agent's fees, body corporate fees, insurances, rates, etc.). Your tax return or notice of assessment will provide details of this. But not all deductions that are allowable for tax purposes are allowable for social security, for example, capital depreciation is not an allowed deduction in this case. If you are not lodging a tax return, your income will be estimated at two thirds of the rental income, less any mortgage interest payments.

Superannuation

It's important to understand how Centrelink treats super-annuation.

CASE STUDY — Ian and Dee

Ian is 67, and his wife, Dee, is 60. Ian was mostly self-employed and did not put much into his superannuation, so the bulk of their assets consist of the family home and Dee's superannuation. As these are both exempt assets, Ian may well qualify for a part age pension.

Dee sought advice about her superannuation, but did not think to mention her family situation or Ian's pension. She was advised to start an account-based pension, which would give her a regular income and reduce tax on her fund's earnings from 15% a year to zero. But it was a bad decision. As soon as Dee started the account-based pension, her superannuation ceased to be an exempt asset; Ian lost his pension and the benefits that went with it.

The fact that the deeming rate starts at just 0.25% means that pensioners should be seeking higher rates. If you look at a research website, such as **Canstar** or **Finder**, you will find a host of financial institutions offering much more than this for deposits, and most share-based investments would do much better than this over the long term.

You have nothing to lose by chasing higher rates — as long as you keep your capital secure — because irrespective of what you earn, you will only be assessed at the current deeming rate. Of course, you then need to spend these higher earnings — if you let them build up in your bank account you may find you've crept over the assets test cut-off point.

Age pension eligibility is a complex topic. It is important to get advice early — for example, Centrelink take into account all money disposed of by gifting within five years of applying for the pension. You can actually submit your claim 13 weeks before you reach age pension age. If you are already receiving an eligible payment, Centrelink will write to you 13 weeks before you reach age pension age and tell you what you need to do to transfer to the age pension.

Working in retirement

If you want to continue to earn some extra money after you retire then you should take note of the Work Bonus. Since 1 July 2019 the Work Bonus allows pensioners to earn up to an average of $300 a fortnight from wages or genuine self-employment before the income is assessed for the pension income test. At the time of writing, there is an extra income credit of $4,000, taking the amount you can earn from $7,800 to $11,800 until 31 December 2023. There are plans to make this higher income threshold permanent from 1 January 2024 (subject to legislation passing).

The government has also introduced other measures to help senior Australians work without getting kicked out of the pension system. These include that pensioners don't have to reapply for their pension payment for up to two years if their employment income exceeds the income limit. It used to be that your connection to social security was cancelled after 12 weeks of exceeding the income limit. You can also retain access to the Pensioner Concession Card and associated benefits for two years.

Pooled lifetime income stream products

The government has been encouraging the financial services industry to develop new retirement income stream products (a form of annuity) that manage the competing objectives of high income, longevity risk and flexibility.

As well as providing increased flexibility for retirees, they can be highly effective for maximising Centrelink benefits in some circumstances. They are complex, so if you are considering investing in them, get expert advice first.

At the time of writing, product providers were in the process of developing new products to meet the changing rules, so from this perspective also, it's important to take advice to find out what's available if and when you think one of these products may be appropriate for your own circumstances.

Major changes in the treatment of these products took place on 1 July 2019. From that date only 60% of the purchase price is assessed for the assets test up to age 84 (or for a minimum of five years) and 30% thereafter. For the income test, 60% of this income is assessed.

The following case study was provided by Challenger, a major provider of this type of product. Just keep in mind that although these figures were correct at the time of writing, rates change continually; the information here is just an example of the kind of thing you may find when you do your research.

> **CASE STUDY**
>
> *A couple, both aged 70, have $800,000 in assessable assets and receive a small part age pension of $4,953/year. If they used $200,000 to purchase a lifetime income product, their assessable assets would reduce by $80,000 (40% of the purchase price) and their pension would increase to $11,193/year, an increase of $6,240/year.*
>
> *Challenger advise me that $200,000 could provide both of them an indexed, lifetime, guaranteed annuity starting at $5,108 per year for him and at $4,796 per year for her (the rates are different because of their different life expectancies). The combination of the increased age pension and the income from the two annuities would give them additional guaranteed income of $16,144 in the first year. That could make a huge difference to their financial situation.*

What if you are not eligible?

We have focused on the age pension, as this is the entitlement most retirees look to claim. But if you are downsizing and are yet to reach age pension age you may need to look at claiming JobSeeker — people aged 55–67 make up the biggest cohort of people claiming JobSeeker. Unfortunately, JobSeeker is significantly less than the age pension, paying only $749/fortnight for singles (increasing to $802/fortnight for people over 55 who have been claiming for nine continuous months) and $686/fortnight for a member of a couple.

Like the age pension, both assets and income tests are applied to work out your JobSeeker entitlement. You will not be eligible to claim JobSeeker if your assets or income exceed the cut-offs.

TABLE 5: *JobSeeker assets and income cut-offs, at 20 September 2023*

Assets test	Homeowners	Non-homeowners
Single	$301,750	$543,750
Couple combined (even if only one is eligible)	$451,500	$693,500

Income test (per fortnight)	Income
Single	$1,431
Single, 55 years of age or older and have been receiving payment for at least 9 months continuously	$1,532
Couple (each)	up to $1,324

Estimating your pension entitlement

If you think you may be eligible for an age pension, you should get advice as soon as possible.

Eligibility for a part pension is of critical importance to many people because it gives access to the prized Pensioner Concession Card — giving you cheaper medical costs and, depending on your location, possibly concessions on utilities, council rates, public transport and vehicle registration — even if the pension itself is a minuscule amount.

The online Age Pension Calculator and Deeming Calculator available through *www.downsizingmadesimple. com.au* are a great starting point. They give a brief overview of eligibility criteria and allow you to enter your own information. *Exercise 9*, below, will help you develop the figures to put into the Age Pension Calculator, or provide information to your financial planner or Centrelink.

You can also visit the Centrelink website. If you work your way through the tabs, most of your questions will be answered. Centrelink offices also offer a free Financial Information Service (FIS) — this can be a good starting point if you have limited resources and no financial adviser of your own. Just know that while they can give you information and tell you what impact a course of action can have on your pension entitlement they can't give you advice: if there is a better way of structuring your finances or a financial product that could help you get more pension it is not their job to advise you.

EXERCISE 9: Pension estimator

	Assets	Assessed income/year
Exempt assets		
House Retirement villages and granny flats are subject to special rules		Fill in all light-coloured fields that apply to your situation, then calculate subtotals.
Funeral bond / Pre-paid funeral, Burial plot		
Total exempt assets		
Personal assets		
Lifestyle assets: Cars, caravans, boats		
Contents, collections, artworks		
Subtotal		

	Assets	Assessed income/year
Investments (not subject to deeming)		
Investment properties / Vacant land		List taxable income.
Account-based superannuation pension/s (grandfathered)		List annual income less deductible amount from annual statement (or Centrelink statement).
Annuities		(as above)
Family trusts / Private companies		List taxable income.
Subtotal		

Daphne, they've sent your assets test back, evidently 'Squillions' isn't an acceptable estimate...

	Assets	Assessed income/year
Investments (subject to deeming)		
		Use *Exercise 8* to calculate your deemed income.
Bank accounts		
Term deposits		
Shares		
Managed funds		
Loans/Excess gifts		
Superannuation		
Annuities		
Subtotal		
Other income		
Wages		
Less Work Bonus		
Defined benefit income		
Subtotal		
TOTAL Add up all the subtotals except the exempt assets.		

If you'd rather have the calculations done for you, use the calculator provided at **www.downsizingmadesimple.com.au**.

Enduring power of attorney

We all have to face the possibility of being aged or sick at some stage. Heart attacks and strokes have no respect for age and can come suddenly, which often leaves a person unable to sign their name to withdraw money that is needed urgently. Please make sure that a trusted relation or friend, as well as your spouse, has an enduring power of attorney that enables them to act for you in the event of physical or mental incapacity. Each state has similar laws, and you will easily find information online about exactly what you need to do to put this important safeguard in place.

5

BORROWING

If you are retiring free of debt, and have no need to borrow, this chapter won't be necessary for you. Congratulations! But if you are still paying off a home or anticipate borrowing to meet future needs, read on.

The most straightforward way to be debt free is to make paying your home off a major focus when you are working, or (next best) to accumulate enough money in superannuation to pay off that loan when you retire.

As a group, Australian retirees have already saved over a trillion dollars that they don't have ready access to: this is the value of the equity in their homes. Indeed, for most households now in retirement, the value of their home equity is more than three times the value of their superannuation savings.

There has been an ongoing quest for products that would satisfy retirees' need for a reliable income stream until they died. In November 2020, the Retirement Income Review handed down a voluminous report that examined the Australian retirement landscape in depth. One of its major findings was that Australians should be prepared to use the equity in the family home as a significant source of their retirement funding. But how can they best do so?

One option is to downsize to a cheaper home, but this strategy often has the major disadvantage of converting an exempt asset — the family home — to an assessable asset. If you are receiving a part age pension now, increasing your assessable assets could severely reduce it, or even totally lose your pension. To make matters worse, the costs of moving from one home to another are high, which usually means a net loss of capital. Most importantly, retirees want to remain in their local communities, and it may be hard to find a good quality smaller home nearby.

One benefit of downsizing is that the government lets each homeowner put $300,000 of the proceeds of downsizing into their superannuation as a non-concessional contribution. But that incentive has not convinced many older Australians to leave their family homes. So not downsizing can leave retirees asset rich, but cash poor.

This leaves two other options: borrow against the home or sell a portion of it using one of the equity release options which are available. Let's look at them in detail.

Reverse mortgages

A conventional mortgage is not a practical option for most retirees. Being asset rich and cash poor, they may not be able to afford the recurring loan payments, and even if they could, most have trouble getting a loan because of their age and lack of paid work. However, there is a product designed for retirement, called a reverse mortgage, for which no regular repayments of principal or interest are required. The loan increases your available income while you live in your home, however the debt also compounds as time passes.

The 2012 ASIC consumer protections provide borrowers using reverse mortgages with guaranteed lifetime occupancy of their homes, full responsible lending protections, and a "no negative equity" guarantee (which means you can't ever owe more than the value of your home). ASIC also put in place conservative loan-to-value limits that increase based on the age of the borrower. For example, at 60 years of age, ASIC prescribes that a reverse mortgage should not be more than 20% of the value of the home. It doesn't sound like a lot, but for many retirees in a $1m home, 20%, or $200,000, would double their superannuation savings. And the conservative ASIC loan-to-value ratios mean that in most economic scenarios, a 65-year-old taking out a loan for the maximum available amount today will retain more than 50% home ownership by the age of 90.

CASE STUDY

A couple aged 75 with a home worth $1 million take out a reverse mortgage of $100,000 at 8.5% per annum. If the home increases in capital value at 3% per annum and no repayments are made on the reverse mortgage, the situation in 15 years would be a house worth $1.55 million that has a loan against it of around $350,000, resulting in a net equity of around $1.2 million.

By this stage the couple would be 90 years of age, and they may decide the house is now too big for them — they may wish to downsize, in which case the debt would be paid from the sales proceeds. Alternatively, they may let the debt keep increasing — secure in the knowledge there is still a large amount of equity which their beneficiaries will inherit tax-free.

Common uses of a reverse mortgage include a monthly drawdown to top up retirement income, or setting one up as a contingency fund for future needs. More and more retirees are now retiring with an outstanding balance on their home loan or credit card, and a reverse mortgage can refinance this debt without depleting retirement income. Another major use of home equity is to renovate the family home to enjoy another 20 years of lifestyle at home and improve the value of a CGT-exempt asset at the same time. Think about it: if you love living where you are, and need $75,000 for home maintenance or upgrades, a reverse mortgage may be a better option than going to all the expense and inconvenience of changing properties.

Perhaps the most important change to reverse mortgages in Australia is that new providers have emerged to deliver home equity as part of individual wealth management and retirement planning, to match retirees' long term plans.

Home Equity Access Scheme (HEAS) (formerly the Pension Loans Scheme)

These reverse mortgages are offered by the Australian Government to older Australians who wish to boost their retirement income by unlocking equity in their real estate assets. Through the HEAS, people can receive regular fortnightly payments, which accrue as a debt secured against their Australian property. The HEAS allows a fortnightly loan of up to 150% of the maximum age pension; for pensioners, this represents around $14,257 per year for singles and around $21,494 per year for couples, on top of receiving a full age pension. A compounding interest rate, currently 3.95%, is charged.

Self-funded retirees can access up to 150% of the full pension — $42,771 per year for a single and $64,483 per year for a couple. Each assessment is based upon the security value and the age of the younger borrower. Initially, the longest loan term is about 13 years, but it can be reassessed each year, with a higher amount possible as a facility, but still capped by fortnightly/annual amounts.

The HEAS is available to pensioners, part-pensioners and non-pensioners. You do not need to be receiving an age pension (or other qualifying pension) from Centrelink, but you still need to qualify by meeting the age and residency rules:

- the property you use as security must be in Australia and adequately insured
- you must be in Australia when you apply
- you cannot be bankrupt or subject to a personal insolvency agreement.

The HEAS is delivered by Centrelink's team of financial information services officers, who don't have to provide all the consumer protections required by ASIC and responsible lending legislation. The properties are revalued annually, and future drawdown availability is adjusted based on valuation, age and a range of other factors.

The May 2021 budget announced a major change to the scheme to make it more user-friendly. As an alternative to drawing the loan fortnightly, people can now access a capped advance payment in the form of one or two lump sums, up to the maximum.

Paul Rogan, of Pension Boost Pty Ltd, a specialist in HEAS, points out that a benefit of a HEAS loan versus a commercial reverse mortgage is that the government will accept any freehold real estate anywhere in Australia. Other lenders are generally constrained to major cities, urban areas and standard houses and apartments. It is therefore particularly good for people in remote postcodes, people with modest home values, and people who have retired early (i.e. before the age of 60).

The low interest rate is attractive, but remember that HEAS has the same issues as any other reverse mortgage: the debt compounds and reduces your capital. Remember that the essence of a reverse mortgage is that no interest or principal repayments are made on the loan, so it increases faster and faster.

A reverse mortgage is not a perfect product, and like a home loan, so much depends on the future of interest rates and home property prices. But in the right situation, drawing part of your home equity can be useful.

Other equity release products

If a reverse mortgage is not quite right for you, what about some of the other options on the market?

DomaCom's pioneering "Senior Equity Release" scheme turns your home's value into shares, some of which are sold to investors. The seller nominates the price, and whether they wish to receive it as a lump sum or a regular payment. On the other side of the transaction, the investor — or investors — buying the shares receive a monthly income of 3%, and a share of the capital value. DomaCom manages payments to the investor/s on your behalf. Maintaining the property and covering ongoing costs like building insurance and rates is shared between the seller and the investor. When the property is sold in full, the seller and investor/s receive their share of the sale price. In the meantime the investor/s also have the option to sell some or all of their shares via the product to another investor/s.

This product overcomes a key drawback of the Home Equity Access Scheme, by allowing homeowners to receive as much of their equity as a lump sum as they wish, not as a lump sum limited to 50% of the annual pension payment. It also overcomes a common issue with other equity release products — there are no restrictions by postcode. This means anyone can get equity release provided there are investors to buy in. And that's the million dollar question with this product: will there be someone willing to buy shares in your home at a price you are willing to sell at?

If you are considering a reverse mortgage or other equity release product, we strongly recommend that you seek advice from the outset. The essence of all these schemes is that you give up some of the equity you may leave to your family in the future, in exchange for money today. Maybe a family member can assist instead, and leave the whole value of the home intact? Of course, for estate planning purposes, any such arrangements need to be documented.

Paying off debt with super

It is quite common to retire with a hefty balance in superannuation and also a debt on your home. Should you withdraw some money from super to pay off the debt or just leave the superannuation to grow, withdrawing money as needed to repay the loan? There is no one-size-fits-all answer. If the interest rate on your home loan is around 4%, and your superannuation is consistently earning a significantly better rate, say 8%, it makes sense to leave the superannuation intact and redraw for home loan repayments as needed.

However, there are other considerations. Suppose a couple, both of pension age and receiving a part age pension, had $600,000 in superannuation and a $200,000 debt on their home. The debt on the home is not offset against the superannuation balance, so Centrelink treats the $600,000 as an asset. By withdrawing $200,000 from super and paying off their home loan, the couple's pension should increase by $15,600 per year because, if your pension is assets-tested, every $100,000 less in assets increases your pension by $7,800 per year.

Borrowing to downsize

Since the 2017–2019 Royal Commission (into Misconduct in the Banking, Superannuation and Financial Services Industry), banks have tightened their lending criteria immensely, and it is currently extremely difficult for a retiree to get a loan. Certainly, if you have a large chunk of money in superannuation and wanted bridging finance to buy a property you may have a chance, but that can be a risky strategy. Many people get caught using bridging finance, because their property does not sell for nearly as much as they expected it to. So it is generally better to stay away from bridging finance and instead sign a conditional contract for a new property, making it subject to completion of the sale of the home you live in now. This too has a drawback — your bargaining position is weaker, so you may pay a little more for the home you are buying.

If you want to enter a retirement community, many won't enter into a conditional contract. A bridging loan is one option that will allow you to move into the village while your home is on the market. But most houses sell according to how they are priced, so if you are keen to grab a good deal in a retirement village, your other option is to lower the price on your home to finalise a sale. You may find it's better to reduce the price of your home and enjoy certainty and peace of mind.

Specialist lenders

Land Lease Home Loans is currently the only financier that provide a loan secured by your home in a land lease community. Before they entered the market, if you did not have 100% of the purchase price the only options available were a loan from family and friends or an unsecured loan from a bank or financial institution. Unsecured loans are often referred to as personal loans; because of their nature (i.e there is no security) the amount you can borrow is often limited to $50,000 and the interest rate is significantly higher than a secured loan — between 10% and 15% per year is common.

Land Lease Home Loans secure their loans over your home in the land lease community and lodge that security interest on the Personal Property Security Register (known as PPSR). The lender also takes a charge over the Residential Site Agreement you have with the community operator, and has a separate agreement with the operator that restricts any transfer of your Residential Site Agreement while the loan is outstanding. This ensures the lender is repaid when the home is sold and protects an incoming purchaser from unwittingly purchasing a home that is encumbered.

A land lease home loan does not benefit from many of the factors that keep traditional home loan rates down, in particular the security being the home and the lease over the land is very different to a standard home. In fact, if you wanted to borrow against your home without the land you would probably find it a very difficult exercise. As a general rule in property valuation, your land is considered an appreciating asset while your home is considered a depreciating asset (property growth occurs because the value of your land increases by more than the value of your home reduces). The standard variable interest rate on a land lease home loan is currently 9.75% per year — which is about 3% more than most home loans, but less than many unsecured personal loans.

Land Lease Home Loans currently offer three types of loan.

1. A 12-month bridging loan secured over your existing freehold property and repaid from the sale. The loan can be used to fund the purchase of your land lease home provided the value of your new home does not exceed 70% of the value of your existing home. Fees and interest can be capitalised, so you don't need to show that you can service the loan, and both principal and interest can be repaid on settlement.

2. A 12-month construction loan to meet progress payments. Instead of taking a single lump sum, this enables you to take multiple payments over a period of time, and has the benefit that you are only paying interest on the funds as you need them. Like the bridging loan, fees and interest can be capitalised and paid on settlement.

3. A traditional principal and interest loan with a term of up to 10 years. Under this loan you can borrow between $20,000 and $250,000, but not more than 40% of your land lease home's value.

The loan amount and term will depend on your ability to afford the repayments, your planned retirement age, and your net worth, that is, the value of your home and other assets less any other debts you have (like car loans, credit cards or investment property loans). In some cases, the loan can be structured to have reduced repayments during its term, with a lump sum payment at the end.

Downsizer bonds

Borrowing to downsize has its benefits: you can buy the house you really want now; depending on the loan you might only have to pay interest, or nothing at all until your home is sold; and you can avoid the hassle and costs of moving twice (paying rent or staying with family or friends while you find your new home). But it also has its downsides: borrowing costs money; interest costs and fees are typically higher than traditional loans; and you will normally need to get at least one, possibly two, property valuations.

Until recently those were pretty much the limit of your options. Now a new option, called a downsizer bond, has entered the market.

A downsizer bond can help you to buy your new home before you sell, by guaranteeing the deposit for you. It's not a loan, it's a guarantee. Unlike a loan there is no loan application or valuation fee, just a simple online assessment. Once you submit the assessment the approval process can be very quick, with approval in as little as 24 hours.

To qualify for a downsizer bond, the net equity in your current home (which is the value of your home less any debt) must be greater than the purchase price of your new home. The term of your bond can be as short as 6 months or as long as 66 months (5.5 years).

If you default on the guarantee because you are unable to settle the purchase of your new home, the seller will sell their property to someone else. If the property is re-sold at a higher price, there is no penalty to you. But if the property is resold for less, you will pay a penalty of the difference, up to a maximum of 10% of the property value.

Let's look at an example.

CASE STUDY

You own a house worth $1,200,000 with no debt. Your equity can get you a new home up to $1,200,000 using a downsizer bond. Although the apartment you want to buy is worth only $800,000, this gives you some equity release and allows for a safety buffer if your current home doesn't sell for what you expect.

The apartment will take 2 years to build — without getting too legalistic, this is known as the "sunset date", which is basically the longest the developer can take to finish the build.

You need to provide a 10% cash deposit, $80,000, today to secure your new home. Using the downsizer bond you can purchase the property with zero deposit for a transaction fee of $1,650 and a bond fee of $4,000 to the guarantee/bond provider, who gives a guarantee on your behalf to replace the 10% cash deposit. Your total cost to transact is $5,650.

In 2 years, you are expected to settle the purchase by selling your home.

However, if something happens and you are unable to honour your contract the vendor will resell the apartment. If the property is sold for at least the contracted price of $800,000 you pay nothing further.

If the property is sold for less than the contracted price, then for each 1% below the contract price you will have to pay $8,000 as a penalty for your non-performance, up to a total $80,000 capped at 10% of the value of the bond.

Any loss beyond the 10% is the responsibility of the downsizer bond provider. In a standard deposit bond, your losses would have been uncapped.

If the developer defaults on the apartment, you will lose the $5,650 you paid, but you didn't pay a deposit, so you won't lose the $80,000 deposit or need to go through a protracted legal process to recover some or all of that money.

If you are considering a downsizer bond so that you don't have to dip into your superannuation or investments, the other thing to think about is whether the cost of the bond is cheaper than losing the interest on those funds. If your investments are earning 4% per year, paying an $80,000 deposit would mean that you are forgoing $6,400 of interest over 2 years. Of course, if your investments are earning more than 4% then the amount you are forgoing would be greater; conversely, if the amount your investments are earning is less than 4%, you really need to think about whether you should just be using those funds.

Hashim @ The Establishment

It is peace of mind for me and for my children ...
Do it, don't wait.

I had a 3 bedroom house with a big front yard and a big backyard, at 82 I found it very hard to maintain. I did have a cleaner come once a fortnight to help me with the inside but I was never really satisfied. I thought that I would be better off with a unit or apartment where I could manage things myself. My daughter kept on saying to me that I need to down-size, "there's no point staying in this big old house that you can't manage" she would say.

So one day I was walking around near Geocon's office and I saw the apartment building they were planning called "The Establishment" so I went in. They gave me the number of the sales person, Dimitri, and he said, "Come in and let's have a chat". I really wasn't sure if I was going to be able to sell my house and with that money purchase an apartment; the new apartments were over $600,000 and I didn't know what my house was worth — I didn't think it would be worth that much, I purchased it 30 years ago for $140,000.

But when I was speaking to Dimitri he said houses in my area were getting more than $1m, so I decided to register my interest in buying one of the apart-ments. I got a real estate agent to value my home and then I got him to sell it. My house sold for more than what I needed for my apartment so I was very happy and my kids were very happy knowing that I could make the change.

I didn't even look at anything else, I bought my apartment off the plan, they didn't even have a display suite at that time but I knew it would be perfect for me — it has 2 bedrooms so I can have one for my study, and 2 bathrooms so I can have one for guests.

Hashim being awarded OAM in 2022

I'm a very active person, involved in community … I hardly have any spare time. Downsizing has let me free up money and time. The biggest surprise was when I moved in with 40 boxes of things: the first couple of weeks I thought "this is too small," as I went through each box, cleaning everything, I realised there weren't enough places to put everything. So I did some renovations, adding floor to ceiling cupboards in the living areas and after 4–5 weeks I started really loving this place, and now I don't want to move anywhere.

My apartment has the most beautiful panoramic view: from my lounge I can see beautiful homes, Yarrabee Pond, and beyond that the hills. I bought my apartment using a downsizer bond, I only paid $1,650 and the sale and the purchase were linked, so it was all done within minutes and they told me it had settled and I moved in. If I hadn't used the downsizer bond I would have had to pay around $67,000, which I would have been in no position to pay and I wouldn't be able to get a loan. Being a Muslim, I found this process where I have some money left over works very well. Borrowing would be hard for me, as charging or paying interest is a taboo in my religion.

My only regret is that, after signing up for my apartment, one real estate agent gave me a valuation that was more than what I eventually ended up selling for, but I didn't go ahead with the sale at that time because my apartment wasn't ready. I guess in hindsight I could have sold and then rented somewhere with the extra money, but I waited until it was ready and then I sold. I'm happy anyway, it was more than enough to pay for my apartment and I still have some money left over to do some other things.

The biggest challenge was dealing with all of the things myself and my late wife had accumulated: I had to get rid of more than half of what we had. I had a few friends who came to help, I gave away some of the furniture because I thought, "I have some spare money, I will buy new things for the apartment". I sold a few things, but mostly I gave my things away. Getting my apartment organised was a bit strenuous: it took me a few months to arrange everything and have it look like a home, but now I have had some friends come over and they say, "Oh wow, this is beautiful".

My advice would be, if you can't manage in your current home then have a look around at apartments and villas, if the price is lower than your home then you can have some money left over and you have more time to spend doing things you like because you don't have to spend all that time on maintaining your home and also it is peace of mind. Peace of mind for me and for my children. If, like me, you don't have enough money to buy before you sell then I would definitely recommend looking into the downsizer bond, then sell the house when you think is the best time. "Do it, don't wait," would be my advice.

I haven't really met any new friends in my apartment building as yet, I mean you see people in the lift and you say hello but then you might not see them for a few weeks. Having said that, when I was living in my house I only really knew the next door neighbours on each side — no-one else. I came to Australia from Malaysia, over there you would know everyone in the village and they would know you.

PART 2:

WHERE TO NEXT?

It's all very well to leave the home you've known and loved, but where should you go next? There are so many downsizing options that the choices can seem overwhelming. Just like people, homes and communities come in all different shapes and sizes. Finding a place that you can call "Home", in a community you want to be a part of, involves research. While you are looking for your new home you may want to turn your mind to what care and support would be available to you if you should need it.

We think it is a good thing to have so many choices — in such a vast range there should be something for everyone — but the price you pay is complexity. You'll need to consider accommodation types, community facilities, lifestyles and activities, as well as the support and care services available if you need them, and of course the legal and financial arrangements that apply. We also show how theory plays out in practice, through many case studies.

In our experience, people who downsize often wish they'd done it sooner. Seize the day.

6

STRATA TITLE HOMES

If the time has come when owning a house on a block of land becomes too much for you, your thoughts will probably turn first to an apartment or townhouse in a strata-title development.

Strata title gives an individual ownership of part of a property, plus shared ownership of the rest of the property through a legal entity, the **body corporate**. Other terms for the same things are "community title", with an "owners corporation" or "community association".

Maybe you are tired of the gardening, tired of the maintenance, or you are looking for a property that you can lock up and forget about for a month or so while you visit all those places that have been on your bucket list for years. For whatever reason, you simply want to downsize to a more convenient property.

However, you may have heard worrying stories about disputes between neighbours, hidden costs and argumentative body corporate members, and wonder if moving to a property where the effective ownership is shared with your close neighbours is the right thing to do.

Every choice has advantages and disadvantages and moving to a strata title property is no exception. The advantages are that maintenance of the common areas is taken care of, the ongoing costs are reasonably predictable, and the property should be in safe hands when you are absent. The disadvantages are potential disagreements with other residents, and unwelcome surprises if you discover that the property has problems.

This is a brief overview of some things to be aware of when you are thinking of moving into a strata title property. It is a huge topic. Just remember, the more due diligence and research you can do, the more likely you are to achieve a satisfactory outcome. Note also that in this chapter we are referring to developments that have already been completed. We regard buying off the plan as high risk, suitable only for very experienced property purchasers.

Don't be downcast by the potential problems we alert you to — every type of property has its pros and cons. Over four million people live in this kind of accommodation and most do so quite happily. Our wish for you is that you join them.

There are three main areas to focus on. We'll call them "private areas", "common areas" and "the local area", but it's not quite as simple as that. We will consider these one by one, and explain their ins and outs as we go.

Private areas

By "private areas" we mean the inside of your new home — the parts that are not seen from outside, and that are maintained by you.

If you have lived in a house for many years, remember to ask yourself whether you would be happy living in an apartment. After all, there are normally some space restrictions, and little garden area. If you are worried about this, a ground-floor apartment or townhouse with its own garden may be a fair compromise. You could also consider renting an apartment for six months to see what you think. We hear stories about people who downsize from a house to an apartment, and after six months decide it wasn't right for them — then have to spend precious capital in moving again.

If you intend to renovate the property, make sure you understand what approvals you may need from the body corporate. Don't rely on a verbal agreement from the manager or committee. It's wise also to check the existing plumbing and electrics fit your proposals, because adjoining neighbours may not take kindly to requests to change the location of services. And if it is a major renovation, check the builders can have somewhere to work from, and how they can remove rubbish from your property.

Know what you are buying

It is absolutely critical that your solicitor does a complete title search, so that what you actually buy is what you think you are buying.

Car spaces and storage areas are where you most often find errors. Your car park is supposed to be noted on your title deed, or in the by-laws, but sometimes the developer has forgotten to record which unit has exclusive use of which car bay on the strata title deed, or re-allocated car spaces to get a sale, without updating the records. Every building has some car spaces that are more user-friendly than others; if changes are not noted on the title deed, a subsequent purchaser may find themselves with quite a different car space to the one they thought they were getting.

So make sure that parking and storage are specifically noted on the title, inspect them to confirm they are suitable, and check where your visitors will be able to park.

CASE STUDY

A great example of title errors comes from some close friends of ours, who had owned a unit in Brisbane for many years. They decided to sell it to move closer to their daughter; they got it under contract to sell, then signed a contract to buy another property, subject to the successful sale of their own.

Both deals went belly up. When the purchasers did their searches, they discovered that my friends' treasured backyard and barbeque area were in fact part of the common property, and their third bedroom was meant to be a common storage area. The contract was cancelled, and my friends spent 18 months and over $10,000 having the title corrected. They had bought it new, and the builder, who has long vanished, had sold them a lemon. Their solicitor had been negligent, but by this time he too was long out of the picture.

Common areas

Common areas include corridors, lifts, driveways, and potentially much more, like a clubhouse, swimming pool or tennis court.

A critical thing to understand about moving to strata title living is that everything that affects the building as a whole, or the outside of the building, is under the control of the body corporate, not individual owners. This applies to any parts of your home seen from outside, such as balconies, some parking spaces, and courtyards.

Take the time to walk around the building and all its functional areas, from the communal gardens to the rubbish facilities. Is the building well-maintained? Are the common areas clean and tidy? Who is responsible for maintenance?

In strata title developments you often live in close proximity to your neighbours, including those who enjoy a very different lifestyle. So look at the design and placement of windows and balconies. Think about how much of their music and conversations you could be hearing, and vice versa. It's also worth finding out whether most of the residents are living there permanently, which gives them a stake in getting on with their neighbours. If there are many short term tenants, they may be less motivated to keep other residents happy.

What you can do is governed by the by-laws, which can be changed by the body corporate, provided they act in a reasonable manner and have majority support. For example, the body corporate could allow budgerigars and cats but no dogs when you move in, then change the rules to allow dogs a few months' later. In many apartment blocks you cannot hang your washing on the balcony where it will be visible. Installing an air conditioner will certainly require body corporate approval, and they will have a say in where it's going to go. In some cases, the body corporate can even change allocated car spaces, but this generally requires a motion without dissent.

Shared electric vehicle charging points would also be common property. As the world is moving to electric vehicles, you'll want to find out exactly where you will be able to charge your electric car when you eventually have one. Many older buildings don't have charging facilities and would have great trouble putting them in, and if you are moving to strata title accommodation this will be a body corporate matter. The key thing is an energy management system (EMS) and the chargers that are installed hooking into that — the EMS slows car charging until outside peak usage times (i.e. 6–9 pm). Unfettered and unregulated charging by anyone with any charger could be a disaster!

Bear in mind that it can take hours to charge an electric vehicle, and you need to ask yourself how long you will be waiting. If, for example, you're living in a 50-apartment building, three chargers are unlikely to meet the demand in a few years.

> ### CASE STUDY
>
> *Despite all your due diligence, unexpected problems can always crop up. Some friends of ours bought an apartment on the third floor of a building at the Gold Coast. When they bought it, the air conditioner was on a ledge outside the lounge room. But when it was time to replace the air conditioner — they corrode quickly when the building is on the beach — the body corporate had passed a special by-law requiring all air-conditioners on the third floor or below to be on the patio of the building. Our friends had to install the replacement air conditioner on the patio, which both reduced their patio space and made it much less pleasant, due to the noise and heat of the air conditioner.*

Reviewing body corporate records

You or your solicitor should contact the administrator of the body corporate — often a large administration company — and do a full search of the minutes and other correspondence relating to the building. This should give you a good indication of potential problems.

A prudent body corporate puts sufficient money into a sinking fund each year to ensure there are funds on hand for repairs and maintenance as the need arises. However, many owners are reluctant to see the body corporate sitting on a large amount of cash in the sinking fund and prefer special levies to be made as necessary. This is unfair to future buyers, because those who have sold and left have not paid their share of the maintenance. Ongoing maintenance can be a major cost, particularly in buildings near the beach where salty air corrodes balcony railings and door tracks.

CASE STUDY

I received the following distressing email from a retiree who'd recently moved into a high rise unit. "Recently I bought a unit in a high rise holiday apartment building — I invested my savings in it and planned to live there for a few years at least. I knew that I would need to do some work on my unit and had budgeted for that. I also knew that I would be able to afford the body corporate fees. But what a shock I got at the AGM.

"The chairman's report reflected many problems with the building that will cost a significant amount to fix. He advised the meeting that the committee kept body corporate fees low to keep the price of units up, and used special levies to meet the major maintenance costs.

"None of this is in the minutes. The committee also seems to have moved away from the sinking fund forecast that was made available in my search of records and they do not have an adequate budget for future repairs. The chairman estimated that about $1,000,000 would be needed for major maintenance. I have been caught out at a time in my life when I just can't afford the special levies."

CASE STUDY

Another reader tells how a search of the body corporate records revealed that the sellers of a property they were considering buying had ignored a request from the body corporate to replace severely corroded railings at a cost of $23,000. The body corporate was forced to carry out the work themselves, at their insurer's insistence, but due to the passing of time, the cost had risen to $48,000. The buyers would have become liable for this cost, so they decided not to proceed.

People are people, so there are many stories in a similar vein. The lesson is clear: before you buy into a strata title, take the time to do a thorough search of the body corporate records and actually read the minutes. These should highlight where potential problems are, and will also give you an insight into the politics of the place. Often the same person's name will crop up again and again — this will be either the stirrer who drives the rest of the owners crazy, or the one with the real power. In either case, try to have a chat with them before you finalise the contract. You will want to make sure you can live with these people before you commit to a long term relationship with them as a co-owner.

Checking for building defects

There are many solidly built and safe townhouses and apartment buildings available, but like all property purchases you must do your due diligence. Don't rely on the word of the seller or the seller's agent — they are not working for you.

At time of writing, there was much publicity about buildings where major defects were just coming to light. It is a challenge, and we are indebted to Michael Teys, a strata consultant who is currently doing a PhD in strata title defects.

Michael suggests five key things you can do to reduce your risk when buying a strata-title home:

1. Buy in an established building at least 10 years old. By this stage any building defects have probably been fixed. Though there may still be combustible cladding and/or problems with water penetration.

2. Ask for a warranty from the seller that there is no combustible cladding on the building. The warranty needs to continue after settlement so you can sue the seller if they've misled you.

3. Do a visual inspection of the whole building to look for cladding that may be combustible. It's easy to spot and there are good videos on the Victorian Building Authority website that will help you identify suspect cladding (but remember the rules for rectification are different in each state and territory).

4. Get your lawyer or conveyancer to check the strata records for any sign of building defects or expensive upcoming maintenance referred to in minutes or reports.

5. Check the history of the strata insurance. Make sure it is current and there has been no significant increase in the annual premiums or excess applicable on claims. Any increase more than 5% in the last year probably indicates there are building defects or suspect cladding on the building.

This is an extra layer of due diligence compared with buying a house, so make sure you look at these strata-specific issues. If possible, chat to as many residents as possible, tell them you're thinking of buying into the property, and ask them what they think of the building and its surroundings.

The local area

Finally, consider the local area — the area outside the strata's boundaries. This needs the same consideration as buying any property, yet it can be easy to overlook, particularly if you are looking at a large strata title property.

Like any property, when you buy strata title you are not just buying an apartment or townhouse, you are buying into the area around it. Take the time to walk around the buildings and adjoining streets, and ask yourself if you would be happy living in this area long term.

In particular, consider the adjoining properties — if nearby blocks have old houses on large allotments it's odds-on that they will also be zoned for multi-dwelling accommodation and you could find yourself suddenly facing months of construction noise, increased traffic, and maybe a loss of views or sunlight, if a large development is approved next door.

Then there's all the usual location questions to consider: transport, shopping, entertainment, and access to services.

Geoff: finding a strata title home

Outside of a retirement community it was very difficult to find an ageing-friendly home.

We decided to downsize because we recognised our ageing frailties and we knew that we need to prepare. The process took about five years — we attended three seminars Rachel and Noel were speaking at: on the Gold Coast, the Sunshine Coast, and in Ringwood, Victoria. We were Grey Nomads who spent winters in Queensland. I was open to staying there — as a Victorian it's easy to get attracted to the northern winters — but my wife didn't want to move away from family.

Our old house, where we lived for 45 years, was two storeys. I had a sore knee from a lifelong love of rowing and marathon running: the stairs and maintaining our home were both becoming hard. I now have a completely new knee, but I'm still very glad we moved to a single level.

I was a financial planner, which was very helpful in navigating the costs and complexity of our downsizing choices. We qualify for a part age pension, and we decided to "supersize" our downsize; otherwise we would have lost our pension altogether. So instead, we tipped a bit of money from our investments into our new home.

We didn't think our lifestyles suited a retirement community, but we were attracted to the facilities, the social aspects: the way of life. We are a couple who like our own company, rather than joining in group activities. Also, Trudy is nine years younger than me, so finding a community where we both felt like we belonged was tricky.

Geoff and his wife Trudy

Our biggest surprise was the lack of options in what we were looking for: outside of a retirement community it was very difficult to find an ageing-friendly home. We spent four years looking for a property with a walk-in shower, wide doorways, and a wide passageway, so that if one or both of us needed a walking frame we could stay at home as long as possible. Demand for this type of house is huge from the baby boomer generation. Twice we were outbid at auction via a telephone bid for the home we wanted: we were told by our agent that in both situations we were up against prospective buyers similar to ourselves.

We ended up choosing a strata home: we share a driveway with our neighbour. We didn't want a battleaxe subdivision, but that's what we have ended up with — we compromised. We wanted something new, but everything we looked at was double storey, and the main bedroom was always upstairs. The few we looked at that had the main bedroom on the ground floor felt cramped. Luckily our agent found us a house that is all one level, on a flat block, with less garden to maintain than our old place, though we still have a front and back yard. Our new home is two doors down from our grandkids' school, so they come to our place every day.

The hardest part was downsizing internally — reducing all our "stuff". I'm a hoarder by nature and we had a lot of storage in our old home. I knew I wasn't going to walk the Kokoda track or hike the high country again, so the tents and hiking gear had to go. Many pieces of furniture we had had since we married 45 years ago we sold. I am a keen woodworker so I had a lot of machinery. Our youngest son is a carpenter so he took what he wanted and the rest I sold on Facebook Marketplace. All up, we recouped $7,000 from the sale of our unwanted stuff.

We have seen friends who are in denial about their ageing: they just won't consider moving. I had dealt with my own mother and knew that acting early was the best plan. We haven't ruled out moving again; there is a development proposal for a village that has care just up the road, which we are keeping an eye on.

Build to rent developments

At the moment "build to rent" is all the buzz for people looking for affordable housing, including retirees.

Build to rent is a popular housing model around the world, which has recently come to Australia. As the name suggests, the developer builds the homes or apartments, retains the ownership and rents them out. The difference between these and other developments that have a combination of individual owners and tenants who rent from individuals, is that these developments are entirely owned and managed by the developer.

Build to rent developments can offer many of the amenities that you would find in a retirement village, such as dog parks, BBQ areas, communal gardens, swimming pools, cinemas and gyms. The fact that the entire development is owned and managed by the developer means that you can have greater flexibility through longer lease terms, lower or no bond, permission to have pets and decorate the home, and the ability to move between homes when your circumstances change. In some cases your rent includes the whitegoods, there are organised social activities, and you can access cleaning and maintenance services through the developer too.

If you currently own your home and are receiving an age pension you need to make sure you know the impact of downsizing into a build to rent development before you make the move. As a non-homeowner, the age pension assets cut-off is $909,500 for singles and $1,245,000 for couples. With the median house price across capital cities currently around $850,000, it is easy to lose your pension if you sell your house and move into a rental. But if you receive the age pension, access to rent assistance of up to $185 per fortnight on top of your pension can help with the cost of your new home.

You need to consider that you don't own the home or have the same security of tenure that you would in a retirement village. You also don't have as much control. In a strata development there's an owner's corporation, which gives you at least some ability to deal with day-to-day running and maintenance of the building and grounds. In a retirement village there is often a resident's committee that represents the interests of residents. In build to rent there's one owner, which can make it easier to manage, but can also make it harder to control rent increases.

Build to rent is often seen as an affordable housing option, and across the eastern states governments are providing incentives to developers to offer some or all of the homes in a development at a lower cost. But that doesn't mean that they are all cheap. In some developments the rent is higher than you would pay in the private rental market, because the development has a lot of amenities or services.

Build to rent can be a great option if you have sold your home but not yet found your next, and if you don't want the commitment of buying into a retirement village or land lease community they could fit the bill. Likewise, if you want to free up all of the equity in your home to spend or invest, then build to rent may suit you. Just remember that the ongoing fees in build to rent will likely be higher than other options — the trade-off is that you don't need to put in a large capital sum.

7

GRANNY FLATS

Granny flats enable multi-generational living in freehold or strata title housing. Families often establish a granny flat to help support one or both parents to continue to live independently; after the death of one parent, for the widow or widower; or when there are clear signs of deteriorating health in one or both parents.

They can be a very attractive arrangement: mum or dad — or both — enjoy their own private space within a property otherwise occupied by an adult child, who is close at hand to provide any help they need. And it can be perfect. Grandparents want to spend time with grandkids; kids are motivated to do the right thing by their parents; and the grandkids are just excited. Having a granny flat can also help overcome social isolation, provide a safer, more secure home that is purpose-built for ageing in place, and save money by pooling the resources of two generations.

While granny flats can be a wonderful downsizing solution, few people realise the complexities that can come with such arrangements. Adjusting to such close living arrangements can be difficult, and people often don't explore their expectations and motivations clearly enough. Parents think their kids will look after them forever; their kids think they are getting a free, live-in babysitter ... What's more, granny flat arrangements embody significant legal and financial issues, including social security implications. It is very important to understand and deal with these at the start, to avoid problems down the track.

Is it a granny flat?

Many people think of a small flat built in the backyard or semi-detached from the main home, which is fully independent with its own kitchen, bathroom and separate entrance.

Source: Funky Little Shack

Source: Funky Little Shack

Source: Funky Little Shack

A granny flat can also be established within an existing home, with or without modifications like grab rails in bathrooms and showers, and ramps to replace stairs.

There are three common ways to establish a granny flat.

1. The parents sell their home and pay for a self-contained unit to be built on their child's property, or for modifications to the child's existing home.

2. The parents remain living in their home and an adult child or children moves in, sometimes with their own family, to provide companionship and care; the parents transfer the title of the home to the child or children in exchange for a granny flat right. If the parents retain ownership of the property, a granny flat right has *not* been established.

3. Both parents and children sell their existing homes and buy a new home in the children's names. If the new home is bought in the parents' names, a granny flat right has *not* been established

While people often refer to a "granny flat right" or a "granny flat interest", legally speaking, there is no such thing. So the document the lawyer draws up could be a "life tenancy", which gives you the right to live in the property, or a "life interest", which gives you the right to use and benefit from the property for the rest of your life. While these two things sound similar, there is a key distinction: one enables you to use the property only to live in, the other means that you can also use the property to create a benefit (normally by renting it out if you are not living there). This can create very different outcomes if you move out, potentially to move into aged care, in the future.

Phil: A solo granny flat with the main house rented

It has been far better than I expected.

I was in a situation where my wife and I had separated. I moved out of the family home and was renting. I decided I didn't want to rent and we had an investment property on a corner block (it used to be our weekender), so I moved in there.

Phil

I spoke to my local council to see what I was allowed to do with the block. They were very helpful, and said that I could build a granny flat (amongst other options, including a child care centre). The granny flat sounded like a good solution, as I didn't really want to knock down the existing house.

I started researching. Initially I was looking at a prefab granny flat that I could just drop on to the land and connect the services — something that was already built. I was quite surprised that the cost was only $40,000 or $50,000 more to get something custom built to fit exactly what I wanted.

I moved into the house while the granny flat was being built, which meant I could keep an eye on the development, and I made a couple of tweaks during construction like adding ducted air conditioning. Once the granny flat was ready I moved in and rented out the original house. It has worked out really well: it gives me some income, which covers a few expenses. I fenced my granny flat in so it's very private, I have separate access with an electric gate, and the home isn't attached, so it's really not like having two homes on a block (except that the boundary fence runs all the way along).

I fleetingly looked at other options, but not really seriously. I knew from previous experience I wanted to avoid body corporates. With everything else going on I wanted to keep it simple. Plus, this property was close to the shops and the village, so it was the right thing for me.

I think the biggest surprise for me has probably been that it is even better than I thought. I was very involved in the process and even though it is a small home it functions just as well as a big home. I have been here since 2020, and I must say it has been far better than I expected.

Phil's granny flat with private entrance and electric gate

There have been a few challenges. Having only a single car space has been one, as I have two cars, and I had to make arrangements for my other car. Storage for my bits and pieces is probably the other thing: I have had to be pretty ruthless about the things I keep. So I rent a lock-up (about 1m x 3m) and that enables me to overcome the storage issue. It's difficult in one sense, but in another sense it's made me realise that I don't really need a lot of stuff, when it comes down to it.

The next door neighbours have just got started building four luxury 3-storey townhouses and have approached me about selling my block so they could develop that too … we will see where that goes.

I think if you're looking into something like this it's really important to contact the council you're in — do your due diligence — because the rules are different everywhere. There's obviously limits to what you can build, even if it's easy to do it. If it's not a prefab home, spend as much time as you can going through all the design and details. I've been involved in real estate and interior design, which helped. It's very much the same process as building a home, just on a smaller scale. But because of that scale it's really critical that you get it right, so it can function well. It's worth investing the time and doing a lot of work in the preliminary stages. I think it's good to keep track of it as it goes along too. I mean, you can't just bowl in while the tools are going, but if you need to, just ask questions.

A few neighbours complained: I painted it almost black, which some people didn't like, and someone else thought that my second driveway wasn't allowed to be there … just little niggly things. There was no real drama, but you just have to know that these things are going to happen. You need to roll with it.

Your homeowner status

Typically, a granny flat right is made within a family: the younger generation provide accommodation in exchange for a payment or transfer of assets. Social security provisions allow people to transfer assets well over the normal gifting limits in exchange for a right to live in a residential property.

Why the special treatment? A granny flat is the principal place of residence for the parents. The amount paid for a granny flat right determines homeowner status and whether the amount paid is exempt for pension purposes. If you are classified as a non-homeowner, then you may be able to claim rent assistance on top of your pension. Centrelink's "extra allowable amount" is the difference between the homeowner and non-homeowner asset thresholds, currently $242,000. If the granny flat right costs $242,000 or *less*, the parents are considered non-homeowners; the amount paid is assessable and they can claim rent assistance based on any rent they pay. Conversely, if they pay *more* than the extra allowable amount, they are classed as homeowners; their granny flat right is an exempt asset and they are not eligible for rent assistance.

TABLE 6: *Age pension homeowner rules for granny flats*

	Amount paid for granny flat right/interest	
	$242,000 or less	**more than $242,000**
Homeowner status	Non-homeowner	Homeowner
Asset threshold	$242,000 higher	$242,000 lower
Assessable assets	includes granny flat	exempts granny flat
Rent assistance	Eligible, based on rent	Not eligible

If a pensioner's former home is sold and replaced by a granny flat right *of the same value*, the asset and income position remain the same, and so does the pension entitlement. But rent assistance could be payable if the amount is less than $242,000.

If a pensioner's former home is sold and a granny flat right bought *for less than the sale proceeds*, the extra money becomes an assessable asset (with deemed income, if the money is invested). If the assessable assets are now over the asset threshold, pension entitlement reduces by $3 per $1,000 of assets. This may not sound like much, but it essentially represents a negative 7.8% return: for every $100,000 over the asset threshold, your pension reduces by $7,800/year.

TABLE 7: Age pension reduction table for assets between threshold and cut-off

Assets over threshold	Pension reduction	Income earned on assets @ 4%
$100,000	$7,800	$4,000
$200,000	$15,600	$8,000
$300,000	$23,400	$12,000

Remember too, that if the assessable assets are financial (bank accounts, term deposits, shares, etc.), even if you are under the asset threshold you must consider the income test. Current income thresholds are $204/fortnight for a single person, which equates to $5,304/year, and $360/fortnight or $9,360/year for a couple. Based on current deeming rates, singles with financial assets over $290,000 (couples over $505,000) and no other income, will find that their deemed income exceeds the threshold, causing a reduction in pension entitlement at 50c per dollar.

If a pensioner's former home and some other assets are sold to buy a granny flat right, pension entitlement would most likely increase. But there are limits to what you can pay, and amounts over the limit will be treated as a gift. Let's look at an example.

CASE STUDY — Jenny

Jenny is 75 and would like to live with her recently divorced daughter, Kate, to help her with the children. Jenny's assets are: house $500,000, cash $500,000, and contents $10,000. She is currently eligible to receive $12,271/ year of age pension.

Option 1: Kate and the kids live with Jenny

If Jenny's daughter and grandkids move in with her, her pension would remain the same. But Jenny's home isn't suitable and nor is Kate's. So Jenny wishes to sell her home and buy a new home with Kate. The value of the new home is expected to be $700,000.

Option 2: Jenny and Kate buy a new home in Kate's name

If Jenny sells her home and pays $700,000 to purchase the new home in Kate's name, this is not considered a gift as she has not paid more than the purchase price of the house. Jenny will still be treated as a homeowner for pension purposes because the amount she has paid is greater than $242,000.

After covering the cost of her granny flat right Jenny is left with $300,000 in the bank, which will impact on her pension entitlement slightly, however the impact is much less than it would have been if she stayed at home — plus both Jenny and Kate get the support they need!

	Stay at home	Granny flat
Age pension / year	$12,271	$27,871
Assets	$1,010,000	$310,000

While this is attractive to Jenny as long as she can live in the granny flat, she also needs to think about how she would fund the cost of aged care in the future, if she needs it. If Jenny has $310,000 of assets when she enters an aged care home, she will be classified as a market price payer — but the market price could easily be far more than $310,000. So she needs to consider, if she did need to move into aged care, where she would want to move to, what it is likely to cost, and how she might pay for it.

How much is too much?

Generally speaking, the amount you pay for a granny flat right is considered, by definition, to be the market price. Because they are family arrangements it can be difficult to place any other value on them. However, if you are a pensioner, Centrelink can apply a reasonableness test to a granny flat right in certain circumstances, such as:

1. You transfer the title to your home (or purchase property in another person's name) plus additional assets.
2. You pay for the cost of construction and transfer additional assets.
3. Centrelink staff have reason to believe you are establishing a granny flat to gain a social security advantage.

Any amount paid in excess of the test would be considered a "deprived asset" (Centrelink's term for gifting in excess

PART 2: WHERE TO NEXT?

of the allowed amounts, e.g. if assets are transferred for less than their market value).

Many people jump to the conclusion that this test will be quite unreasonable, but actually it may allow you to transfer significantly more to your children then the construction costs, without penalty.

The reasonableness test amount calculation

Maximum annual couple pension* x Conversion factor** = Reasonableness test amount

* As at the date the granny flat right was established and regardless of their actual pension entitlement.

** The conversion factor is based on age (see Table 8). When calculating the amount for a couple the age next birthday of the youngest member is used.

Note: This test excludes the extended land use test, which enables people on farms to exempt more than the principal home and 2 hectares of land provided they meet certain criteria. For the reasonableness test the adjacent land above 2 hectares can be considered the transfer of additional assets.

EXERCISE 10: Your reasonableness test amount

	Your result	Notes
Age next birthday		Couples use the age of the youngest person
Conversion factor		Copy from *Table 8*, depending on your age
Couple combined pension	$42,988	Update if necessary, at *www.downsizingmadesimple. com.au.*
Reasonableness test amount	$_____	Conversion factor x couple combined pension

If you'd rather have the calculations done for you, use the calculator provided at **www.downsizingmadesimple.com.au.**

TABLE 8: Reasonableness test amount conversion factors according to age

Person's age next birthday	Conversion factor	Person's age next birthday	Conversion factor
51	33.94	76	12.78
52	33.02	77	12.07
53	32.09	78	11.37
54	31.18	79	10.70
55	30.27	80	10.04
56	29.37	81	9.41
57	28.47	82	8.80
58	27.57	83	8.21
59	26.69	84	7.65
60	25.80	85	7.11
61	24.92	86	6.60
62	24.05	87	6.13
63	23.18	88	5.68
64	22.33	89	5.26
65	21.48	90	4.87
66	20.64	91	4.52
67	19.80	92	4.19
68	18.98	93	3.89
69	18.16	94	3.63
70	17.36	95	3.40
71	16.56	96	3.19
72	15.77	97	3.01
73	15.01	98	2.86
74	14.25	99	2.72
75	13.50	100+	2.60

But wait, there's more! And it doesn't involve the reason-ableness test, but may lead to the value of the granny flat right being considered a deprived asset. If an older person needs to vacate a granny flat within five years of it being established *and the reason that they need to leave could have been anticipated at the time the granny flat right was established,* the value of the granny flat right can be considered a deprived asset.

CASE STUDY — Pearl

Pearl is 77, she has a house worth $600,000, plus $20,000 of investments and $5,000 in personal assets. Pearl currently receives the full age pension of $28,514 per year.

She needs some assistance and would like the company of family, as she finds herself lonely since her husband passed away.

Option 1: Pay the construction cost

If Pearl sells her house to cover the cost of constructing a granny flat ($200,000) in her children's home, she will be considered a non-homeowner; the amount she has paid will be included in her assets, and she can qualify for rent assistance. The remaining $400,000 from the sale of her home will also be included in her pension assets. Her pension will reduce to $22,177/year, but she may be able to receive up to $4,805/year on top of her pension in rent assistance. This option also gives her $420,000 to invest or spend.

Option 2: Pay more than the construction cost

If Pearl pays for the construction costs ($200,000) and also gives her children $300,000, her granny flat right will be compared to the reasonableness amount of $488,778 (annual couple's pension $42,988 x 11.37 (conversion factor for age next birthday of 78)). So, although Pearl has paid

$500,000 for her granny flat right, Centrelink would treat the "reasonableness test amount" of $488,778 as her cost; the remaining $11,222 would be considered a gift. The gift amount is added to her other assets of $125,000, but the total of $136,222 is below the asset threshold for the age pension, so Pearl receives the full age pension. Because she has paid more than $242,000 for the granny flat, she will be treated as a homeowner and won't be eligible for rent assistance.

	Assets remaining	Pension/year
Pay construction cost of $200,000	$425,000	$22,177 + rent assistance up to $4,805
Pay $500,000 with reasonableness amount of $474,174	$125,000 + $11,222 gift	$28,514 + no rent assistance

Capital gains tax (CGT)

The tax treatment of granny flats was changed on 1 July 2021. But accountant Julia Hartman, a well-recognised expert in property tax law, points out that there are still a few tax issues to be aware of.

So what's changed?

Before 1 July 2021, the ATO considered a lifetime right to reside as an asset the child would be "disposing of" to their parent/s: this was a D1 capital gains tax event. Essentially, the asset was treated as having been created at the same time as the occupancy right, so the asset had not been held for more than 12 months before it was sold, which meant the 50% CGT discount did not apply. Because the transaction is not arms-length, the parent is always deemed to have paid market value. The capital gain is then calculated by deducting the cost base from the "sale" proceeds. But in the case of a granny flat right, the only expense that makes up the cost base is the legal fees to draw up the agreement. The cost of building the granny flat does not go into the cost base.

Even if the parent paid nothing, the ATO would insist on a market value being calculated based on what it would cost to obtain this right somewhere else, or by using a discounted cash flow of rent over the life expectancy of the parent.

After 36 years of this insanity, the government finally changed the law from 1 July, 2021.

CGT on a lifetime right

You still need to be careful to ensure you fit within the new concession, or the children will have this deemed CGT event as described above. The agreement must meet the following requirements:

1. The parent needs to be over age pension age, or disabled for at least the next 12 months.

2. The property must be a dwelling, and be owned by an individual — not a company or a trust.

3. No rent can be charged, though the parent may contribute to the running costs of the property.

4. The right to occupy is intended to be for the life of the parent, but it can have termination or variation clauses, for example, moving to a different property.

5. The agreement must be in writing and clearly show that the parties agree to be legally bound by it.

6. The agreement can set conditions for money to have to be repaid by the house owner. Tax does not apply to this transfer back to the granny flat occupier.

7. It does not have to be a child–parent relationship, it can be friends, etc., just as long as it is individuals on both sides of the contract.

8. The person granting the granny flat right does not have to be living in the property, in fact the granny flat right can be for the whole property. But as the granny flat occupier cannot give their main residence exemption to the property (because it is not in their name) such a property may be exposed to CGT on sale.

While it's not a good idea to avoid a written agreement, if you don't establish any rights in writing you do avoid triggering a CGT event. It is the very existence of a granny flat right that could land the house owner with a CGT liability, so if you are going to do one make sure you get it right.

Shirley:* Living close to my son has been the easy part

Poor advice has made this stressful and expensive.

We were living on the south coast of NSW. Other than our house, which was worth $690,000, we had a small investment portfolio and we lived on a part pension.

I lost my husband in 2014 after a long illness ... After Jack died, I thought about downsizing, but I really wasn't sure what I could afford and whether a retirement village would be the best option — in hindsight I think maybe it would have been.

So I was 77, recently widowed, and supporting my daughter in Sydney who was going through a relationship breakdown. I was travelling there every week or two to help out and to spend time with the grandkids, who I adore.

When I went to speak to someone at Centrelink, they said that a granny flat would be the ideal solution: that I could spend anything up to $406,000 and that it would "solve all my problems". I had two or three meetings with my local Centrelink office ... they gave me a report and some other information about granny flat arrangements. It suited me to move in with my son. I asked Centrelink if I needed an agreement and they just said, "Some people do, some people don't — it's up to you. But if you do get an agreement, bring us a copy to put on your record".

My son has a friend who is a lawyer and he helped us put together a basic, one-page agreement and I took that to Centrelink. I sold my house and paid my son the $406,000 Centrelink said I could.

To our shock, when my son did his tax return the following year his accountant flagged that our granny flat agreement was going to create a $200,000 tax bill.

It wasn't until this point that we got specialist legal advice and discovered that the way our agreement was worded could be viewed as my son granting me a "property right". To the tax office, this would mean he sold and acquired an asset on the same day: one that attracts capital gains tax!

We have created a new agreement and we are still waiting to hear whether or not this is accepted as a granny flat agreement and not one of these "property rights". All in all it has been an incredibly stressful experience and — depending on the outcome we get —potentially a very expensive one too.

I think Centrelink should make people aware that these arrangements are not as simple as "Spend anything up to $XXX"; you need to set them up properly.

The lady I spoke to at Centrelink told me that she recommends this to lots of people. I shudder to think how many find themselves in our position.

* Names and other identifying factors have been changed at "Shirley's" request.

Joint assets included for aged care assets assessment

An alternative to having a contract is for the parent to just buy into their child's home; as we pointed out earlier, from a Centrelink perspective they then wouldn't have a granny flat arrangement. From a tax perspective, as long as the home has always qualified for the child's main residence exemption, there will be no CGT payable on this transfer, although stamp duty may apply. This gives the parent a legal right to occupy, while covering their share of the property with their main residence exemption.

If the title is a joint tenancy, when the parent dies the ownership reverts back completely to the child without any CGT consequences. Further, other heirs cannot challenge that part of the parent's estate. On the other hand, if the title is held as tenants in common, it can allow some of the money paid for the granny flat to become part of the parent's estate, which may allow another sibling to have some rights in the event of the parent's death.

But with either type of co-ownership, the value of the parent's interest in the home can be included in their aged care assessable assets, with implications for the age pension, and for the cost of residential aged care if needed in the future.

CGT at sale on a separate dwelling

The next important consideration with granny flats is to make sure it is not considered a separate dwelling from the main house. If it is, then the child's main residence exemption will not be able to protect any capital gain on the granny flat. The ATO takes a rather strict view on this (in TD 1999/69). Even if you are all related, unless you are in and out of each other's homes frequently and eat together more than once a week, the granny flat will be considered a separate dwelling.

Repossession risk

Once a granny flat becomes fixed to the land, it is owned by the owner of the land. The problem of multiple dwellings and/or ownership rights may be solved by a using relocatable home, or tiny house on wheels. The parent can buy that and still own it, because it is considered an asset separate from the land. While the child would not be able to give their parent/s any legal right to park the dwelling on their property without triggering CGT, at least the parent gains some sense of security from knowing that they can relocate the home if necessary. This is also an excellent idea if the child's home is mortgaged, as a mere occupancy right does not override a bank's right to repossess the property. A relocatable home is not part of the property, so it at least could be retained.

What happens later?

Children and parents may start off with the best of intentions, but they are often working on the basis of unspoken expectations. Too often they realise the differences in these expectations when confronted with a new situation months or years down the track. Typically, these situations are ones that could have been foreseen but were not considered, and it turns out that people's expectations of what would happen in that situation are completely different.

For example, what will happen when the children wish to go on holidays, if the parent/s cannot manage without them? What will happen if the parent's care needs change and they cannot be safely looked after in the home? Who should pay for the cost of care? Will the parent/s contribute to household expenses such as food, utilities and insurance? The living arrangement may continue for many years, so what happens if the adult children divorce, or if one of those caring for the parent/s becomes ill, or even dies? What about if the parent/s remarry?

In many cases the purchase of the granny flat right is funded from the sale (or transfer) of the family home. Disputes often arise among siblings. Children who concede that they are unable or unwilling to live with their parents still have a vested interest in the family home as the largest asset in the future estate.

To try to please everyone, a parent may decide to transfer only part of the value of the home to the child they live with, and amend their will so that the value they retain passes to the other children in due course. But the child living in the house may later find themselves both bereaved and homeless, with siblings keen to sell their share of the home as fast as possible. So think ahead, and explore possibilities. With some flexible thinking and willingness to negotiate, granny flats can be a wonderful way to downsize.

Narelle: Two generations on the one block

Get the combo right and it works well.

My husband and I moved from our 4-bedroom place up in northern Queensland to Brisbane because our eldest daughter had a baby, and she wanted to start a business and buy a house. It's so hard for kids these days to pay rent and save a deposit to buy a home of their own. The hardest part I think, for the kids, was chasing the property market: it just kept going up and up and they were saving as hard as they could, but they couldn't keep up with the market. I looked at what was happening and I thought, "It's not about how hard you work to get ahead, we need to pool our resources".

So we sold our house and bought a house on a big block that we could build a granny flat on. We were able to pool our resources so the kids didn't need to save a deposit, they could just come straight in and start paying off their mortgage. The block is on a corner, so their house faces one street and our granny flat faces the other street. This means we have separate entrances, which is great, but at the same time we are all together and I get to help raise my grandson, which is wonderful.

At first we all lived in the existing home, then when I retired I took out my super and we built a 2-bedroom granny flat. We have a mortgage too, we are all on that, and as far as the bank is concerned we are all responsible. But to make it fair we went to a solicitor and we got a document drawn up to say that if the worst was to happen and they didn't make their payments then they are responsible. We were able to split the loan so we pay our share and the kids pay theirs.

We own the home as tenants in common: my husband and I own 50% and our daughter and her partner own the other 50%. When we fall off the perch our share gets divided up with our three other kids; if my daughter wants to keep it, she can pay out the others, or they might decide to rent it out, or their kids might move in here ... Whatever it turns out to be, we discussed it amongst ourselves and with the other kids and the solicitor and everyone is happy with it. It's a lot of fiddling to get it all documented, but everyone gets a roof over their head and everyone is happy, and those are the main things.

It's great security for my daughter and I as well. Her husband is working fly-in fly-out in the mines and my husband is on night shift, so it's nice to have someone else around when the boys are away. Having a bigger property has meant my daughter can run her photography business from home; she built a big shed that she uses as her studio and to run her business.

I think the hardest part is the actual living together: learning that the kids are actually adults and we can't tell them what to do any more! We share a lot of things: my husband mows, they take care of the pool. We share the rates and we pay a third of the electricity (because we use less). It works quite well, and if you run out of something you can always duck next door and say, "Have you got an onion?" We worked it all out — what we are all responsible for — upfront, in a big family discussion. Some things have come up that we didn't plan for, like, we needed to get some trees removed and we paid for that because that was on our part of the land.

Narelle and her family

We didn't have all the drama of building a house, from the point of view of council approval we deliberately built under the threshold so we don't get charged extra rates and the process was really easy.

In our council it's all about how big the dwelling is under the roof. You can have a deck as big as you like, but you have to keep under a roof size of 100 m².

We paid to replace the old septic system with a home sewage treatment plant, which recycles the washing machine water so you can use that to water your plants and flush your toilets. We are on town water but we then recycle that. The company comes out every three months to service it and put in the chemicals to keep it all running. It's probably cheaper than having the septic emptied every so often and we don't have the risk of nasty smells.

We have been here five years. It's been easy for my daughter and I to live together, because we have for so many years and we know how it works, but the two boys? They had to find their groove.

I think, if you're thinking about doing something like this you need to sit down with your kids and talk to them; nut out the issues. Make sure their partner — if they have one — plans to stick around ... Not everyone can live with one another, so I think you should do a trial: have the parents come and stay for a while ...— Can you get along? Can there be two lions in the den?

Then you need to think about what you want to buy: how much space you need will determine how much land you need. The biggest thing, of course, is if you have a loan make sure everyone keeps up to date with their payments. If they think, "Mum and Dad will cover me," and they don't pay, it's your good name that's being pulled down. I used to work in the bank, so I taught my kids they have to keep up their end of the deal and make their repayments.

Living here means I probably won't have to go to a nursing home and I'm not socially isolated if my husband dies or vice versa. Don't go into something like this if your kids want to have a good time all the time and have lots of debt: that's not going to work. But get the combo right and it works well.

Keep calm and get professional advice

For all these reasons, it really is important to seek legal and financial advice to help you set up the right agreement, whether as a parent or child, and to provide certainty and transparency on the details.

Although Centrelink does not require a legal document to accept that a granny flat right has been established, they do recommend that people consult their solicitor and perhaps have a document prepared to give evidence of the arrangement. It might seem strange to have a legal document to protect your rights in a family matter, but it could save problems and unpleasant arguments down the track.

EXERCISE 11: Granny flat checklist

Legalities:

☐ When does the agreement begin?

☐ What accommodation will be provided?

☐ If this property is sold will the granny flat arrangement transfer to another property?

☐ Have you checked state and local planning laws to understand what can be built?

☐ Is there any requirement to reinstate the property, i.e. remove the granny flat, when it is no longer occupied (e.g., under Victoria's Dependent Person's Unit rules)? If yes, what is the estimated cost of reinstating the property, and who will pay it?

Finances:

☐ How much is being paid?

☐ Is there any tax liability? How much is it?

☐ Is there any residual value when the parent/s leave? How is it calculated?

☐ Will rent be charged? How will this be calculated over time?

☐ Who will pay what towards household expenses such as utilities, rates and insurance? How is this calculated?

☐ What about living expenses, particularly food costs?

☐ Will the children need insurances such as trauma and/or life insurance to pay out any mortgage if anything happens to them?

Lifestyle:

☐ What assistance will be provided now and in the future? Remember to consider this in both directions.

☐ Who will do what towards running the household, i.e. mow the lawns, clean, wash dishes, do laundry?

☐ What will happen if the children want to go on holiday?

☐ What will happen if the children get divorced?

☐ What about if the parents get divorced or a single parent remarries?

☐ What would happen if the children became ill or passed away?

☐ If care is needed: Who will provide it? How much will be provided?

☐ If more care is needed, i.e. care services in the home and/or respite services, who will pay for it? (See Part 3 to explore the range of government-funded and private care services.)

Here's the hardest part. While everyone moves into these arrangements with good intentions and high hopes for a harmonious intergenerational living arrangement, at some point it will end. It may be because there is a breakdown in the family or because the parent or children pass away or because the arrangement is not able to provide appropriate accommodation or care.

At the end:

☐ What are the circumstances under which the agreement can end?

☐ Does the parent have any residual rights in the property,
i.e. does the agreement allow them to rent the property out while they are living elsewhere?

☐ Have the wills of all parties been reviewed to reflect the agreement?

☐ Have powers of attorney and advanced medical health directives been reviewed in light of the agreement?

If you need more space, draw your own columns on any piece of paper, or download a smart PDF to print or type into from www.downsizingmadesimple.com.au.

Anne: My future-proof house at my daughter's

I knew it was going to be good, but it's been just marvellous.

It was a pretty simple decision for me: when my husband got sick we moved to town off 6 acres down near Byron Bay. We got a beautiful high set Queenslander with 3 bedrooms, 2.5 baths, a formal lounge, dining room … the whole shooting match.

My husband passed away suddenly and I found that I just used the kitchen, bedroom, bathroom and laundry. I thought, "Well I can cope living like this — just me myself and I". Then I had my hip replaced and I was commuting every few weeks to the Gold Coast to see my daughter … it was getting hard. I had a beautiful garden, but it needed too much maintenance so I got a lawn mowing man, and I was struggling to clean such a big house so I got a cleaner to help me, but all that costs money.

My daughter suggested building a granny flat in her backyard. It was actually very quick and easy to get it all certified and have the plans approved by the council. I wasn't completely happy with the original design, but my daughter has a friend who is a project manager, and he found Mel from Funky Little Shack. Mel designed the whole thing within the parameters of what had already been approved, then we tendered for a builder and Mel supervised him.

I'm so happy with my little house! The powerpoints are high up, so I don't have to bend down to plug anything in; I have high windows at the back so I can get the breeze but can't see neighbours (and they can't see me). My bathroom is just magic — I have beautiful Italian marble, but it's been designed in case I need a wheelchair (in fact my whole house has been). There's a beautiful walk-in shower, wide doorways, and anchors in the walls for a grab rail, which I'm just about to get put in.

I thought about buying a unit, but doing it this way was a bit cheaper and that gave me some money to go travelling, plus I'm close to my daughter, and if I'd bought a unit it wouldn't have been future proof in terms of mobility. I'm not the sort of person who needs entertainment all the time — I can adjust and live alone — but together we form a lovely family. We often share dinner, and on the weekend we go out for breakfast together.

I knew that being in a different environment and having my daughter close by was going to be good, but it's just been marvellous. Of course she has her own friends, and I'm starting to make my own group of friends now, and I'm thankful the covid lockdowns are over so I can visit my old network in northern NSW again too.

I think the biggest challenge has been the traffic. I came from a small town where it took half an hour to get down the main street because you know everyone, but there was only one set of traffic lights.

I had to get used to city life, but I would never go back to a small town again. I have everything I want at my fingertips here: I'm close to the shops, hospitals and cafés.

Anne (right) and her daughter

We jokingly call my house "Balmoral," because it's where the Queen lives, and my daughter's house is "the servants' quarters"; it's just one of the many little jokes that we have.

It works well for us. It's comfortable and affordable; we share all the bills and it runs smoothly. But you do need to think about what you want and need now and in the future.

8

COLLABORATIVE HOUSING

Collaborative housing describes a community in which residents have input into the design and management of their community. Typically, residents have a say about which parts of the property are private and which are for communal use, and community members often share other resources too, such as cars, trailers, gardening tools and equipment. Decisions on sharing spaces within the building/s need to be made during the design process, but other decisions — such as how often residents get together to share a meal or work on community projects — can evolve throughout the life of the community. Almost all collaborative housing communities share outdoor spaces, storage and parking, often with carpooling, most have a shared space for eating together and possibly a shared kitchen or barbeque area, but generally each household also has its own self-contained kitchen and dining area.

Some might call them "hippy communes", others may say that they are only for the young, but the reality is that various types of collaborative housing appeal to a broad range of people who want to be part of a community, whether it's big or small. If you think about it, a granny flat is a small-scale collaborative housing arrangement. Collaborative housing often appeals to people who are conscious of their ecological footprint, want to live within their means (physically and financially) and are happy to take on duties beyond just paying money to maintain both their home and the community it is situated in.

Understanding all of the options in the spectrum of collaborative housing is no mean feat, and we are indebted to both Professor Chris Riedy and Caitlin McGee from the Institute for Sustainable Futures at the University of Technology Sydney for their insights and research. To explore the many options further we recommend the website *www.collaborativehousing.org.au*.

At the heart of collaborative housing is the idea of sharing. Sharing has a number of benefits from saving money on the development cost due to not replicating rooms and facilities through to building a sense of community and being eco-friendly.

There is a full spectrum of collaborative housing, from extended families sharing a city block, to full ecovillages. A small collaborative housing venture may mean two or three homes sharing a suburban block; a large one may be an apartment building housing dozens of residents … All offer shared common areas and community activities.

One form of collaborative housing popular in northern Europe is a small cluster of homes around a common house. This model also works in apartments with common areas rather than a separate building. The common house/area typically includes the shared kitchen, dining and lounge space — many co-housing residents say the shared meals are an essential part of building a strong community. Depending on group interests, the common house might also include facilities like workshops, art studios and bookable guest accommodation. The private homes are generally small, due to the shared facilities available.

This could be the start of something …

There is a common process for developing collaborative housing, and you can seek help from those already working in the space at every step of the way.

1. Find your "tribe". If it is family or friends then you are already there, but if you are looking at joining an existing or emerging community then Cohousing Australia (*www.transitionaustralia.net/site/cohousing-australia/*) can help connect you. Or if it is a bigger development in a metro area then the developer may find your tribe for you.

2. Have a plan. What will be private? What will be shared? How will the shared facilities be maintained?

3. Have a contract. Understand any limitations on borrowing and the ability to enforce rights and responsibilities. Make sure you understand the financial capacity of the group, as well as what each individual person's equity

is or will be. Look into the protocols of the community around how decisions are made.

4. Develop. You will normally need local government approval, an architect or designer with experience in collaborative housing, and a reputable builder. If you're doing something on a larger scale then you may be best partnering with a developer who has the skill and experience in land acquisition, feasibility modelling and selling.

5. Enjoy your responsibilities, as well as the benefits.

Ownership options

There are a range of different legal contracts used in collaborative housing.

• **Strata title or community title:** These allow for a combination of private ownership over the private residence area and shared ownership of communal spaces. Strata title is generally used for apartments, and community title for housing estates.

• **Company, unit trust or cooperative ownership**: These structures give ownership to a company, trust or cooperative with residents being shareholders, unit holders or members of the entity — which gives them the right to live in the dwelling and use the common areas.

• **Joint ownership**: This model gives residents title over the property. Joint ownership means that everyone owns all of the property and the "last one standing" owns it all (*not*, as many people believe, that you own something in equal shares with another person or group of people).

- **Tenants in common:** This model gives residents title over the property, and their legal interest in it is expressed in percentage terms. For example, they may own 33%, if the property is owned three ways, or 25% if it is owned four ways — under this model you can also have differences in equity, such as one owner may have 50%, while the other two each have 25%. You can sell your share in the property (subject to any restrictions in your contract) and bequeath it as an asset through your will.

- **Rental:** Unlike other private rentals in the marketplace, renting within a co-housing development may require you to become a member of the cooperative (membership fees can vary widely). As a member you are responsible for abiding by the rules of the cooperative. There may also be other restrictions in place, for example, housing under this model may be restricted to people with limited financial means, who need accommodation closer to medical treatment or who are escaping domestic violence. Some communities have a combination of homes to rent and owner-occupied homes.

Of course, the implications of your ownership extend beyond the right you have to live in the community and how community rules are created and enforced. Some important considerations for your contract include:

- What rules, if any, exist for buying into the community, selling your home, renting the property out, or bequeathing it through your will?

- Can you borrow against your property? In a strata development, for example, it is usually quite easy to borrow, but it is more complex if you are joint tenants or tenants in common.

- What future proofing has been undertaken? What happens if a resident dies, divorces or has a change of circumstances and wants to live elsewhere? What happens if someone needs aged care? Are there circumstances in which you can be obliged to move within the community or to leave the community altogether?
- How are rules created and changed in relation to the governance of the community?
- What are each person's rights and responsibilities?

Heather @ The Shedders

You really need to be willing to communicate and have a shared vision.

The conversation started in around 2001. At the time, the six of us were all holidaying together for a couple of weeks at Christmas — something which had become a tradition that we looked forward to as we enjoyed it so much.

We were talking about what we would like our retirement to look like. We reflected on what retirement looked like for our parents and knew we didn't want that: we saw them stay in the family home and become increasingly isolated and unable to maintain it. We decided we would be happy for our retirement years to be like our holidays and realised that we were getting serious, so we decided that we should "sleep on it" for a while.

In April that year we met up with big sheets of butcher's paper and brainstormed what it would look like — the upsides and potential issues. Since that meeting, we have had a vision and we have kept that vision ahead of us all the time, which has helped us overcome our many day-to-day obstacles.

Creating our home has enabled our savings to stretch better: we have 4 acres and beautiful, big gardens, which none of us could have afforded individually. We only need one washing machine, dishwasher and kitchen and we share utilities and rates — I estimate our running costs are about half of what we would pay living on our own. But the most important thing is that we have this beautiful home within a supportive community.

We have lots of challenges too — day-to-day dynamics of six people with different perspectives can be interesting, so agreeing to things as small as a kettle or as big as a renovation can be challenging.

The house itself has three suites — one for each couple. Within each suite is a good-sized sitting area (we use ours as an office), a large bedroom, a full bathroom and a deck. Jointly we share a music area, lounge room, kitchen, and of course the gardens.

I personally thought I would need more privacy and maybe have a kettle and toaster in our suite, but actually it's lovely to be able to stumble into the kitchen in the morning, and more often than not someone has already got the kettle on.

We did our homework: for two years we rented a large home in Sydney where we each had a floor, so we got to try things out. Again, I originally expected that we would cook our own meals, etc. but we didn't — we shared those things and it was lovely.

The Shedders (L–R) Heather, Daniel, Judy, Rick, Michael and Eve — in their home

When we decided to build, we engaged John Basden of Sunergy Design in Nabiac, who is a designer, not an architect, to show us some of his designs. He is a fascinating character, and he found what we wanted to do a challenge! He developed a design that incorporated what we wanted — which included a fireplace, a number of living areas, and plenty of privacy in the living quarters. We didn't need to borrow to fund anything: we made that a condition of the agreement so that no-one's debt could fall back onto the rest of group. You see, we jointly own the property. It took us a while to nut out the exit agreement — we thought through all the things that could possibly happen, like the death of one spouse, divorce, changing priorities (such as moving closer to family) the need to move to aged care … We came up with a very simple arrangement whereby the other owners have the first right to buy; if one couple say no then the other couple can buy all of that share, but if they say no then we sell that share to a new couple, and if no buyer could be found then the house would be sold. The total process could take up to a year.

We each used our own lawyer. And we have all put in our wills a direction to our beneficiaries to leave the home alone until there are only two people left remaining in it — of course it's not legally binding, but we have also spoken to the children about it.

Co-housing is a spectrum of closeness. At one end, people live independently but have shared facilities that make it a community; we are at the other, more "intimate" end, where we are coming into contact with each other every day. In my view we pay the highest price — I mean in terms of social effort — we organise everything by consensus: there is no voting, no 51% majority. It often means a lot of discussion and negotiation. Consensus may not be sexy but it's foundational to making our community workable long term.

If you're thinking about this, you really need to be willing to communicate and have a shared vision. Every meeting (and there were hundreds) we spent a few minutes talking about what it would be like. You need that shared vision and you need a willing-ness to talk about money and to solve any issues.

Narara Ecovillage

Ecovillages are typically the largest, in terms of land size, in the collaborative housing space, so they tend to be in rural areas or on the suburban fringe. The greater land size typically means more residents, but it doesn't necessarily mean bigger houses.

Narara Ecovillage sits on a 63-hectare site on the Central Coast of NSW. When we wrote the first edition of *Downsizing Made Simple*, there were around 180 people living in the community; there are currently almost 240, with around half living on the site. Ages of community members range from newborns to early 80s, including about 60 children. The community plans to grow to just over 300 people in around 150 homes that occupy only 20% of the site. Agriculture and common gardens are allocated another 20%, and the rest will be retained as native bushland.

Community members are diverse, including plumbers, bankers, property valuers, landscapers, social workers and midwives; what they all have in common is the goal of living in a more socially, culturally, economically and eco-logically sustainable way. The development has received a federal government grant to fund an innovative smart solar grid. Narara will manage its own drinking water, stormwater and sewage systems, and buildings must meet stringent sustainable building standards.

Stage 1 includes 42 house blocks and 18 townhouses. There are also more than 50 existing structures — from when the site was the Gosford Horticultural Institute — which are being repurposed to form a visitor centre, offices and communal greenhouses, sheds, garages, and workshops.

Stage 2 is currently selling. The village holds open days and other events regularly, to give people the opportunity to explore the ecovillage, discuss collaborative housing options and get further information: *www.nararaecovillage.com.*

After doing their due diligence, prospective residents first join the cooperative, by purchasing 30,000 shares at $1/share, which gives access to the shared land and facilities. Memberships can be shared as well. They also agree to build on their lot and contribute 52 hours' work each year to help the cooperative. If a member wishes to leave, they sell their home in the usual way with just one caveat: the buyers must also join the cooperative.

Mary-Faeth @ WINC (Older Women in Cohousing Inc.)

We are designing for interaction and community, sustainability and accessibility.

We founded WINC CoHousing (older women in co-housing) because quite a few women we knew didn't have a lot of superannuation or financial resources, and needed some assistance to secure long term housing. Women often also face social isolation, because they have to move far away from friends due to costs. We saw the opportunity for a cohousing development to provide the financial and community benefits that come from living together and sharing.

Mary-Faeth

Our community was founded by women who identify as lesbian, though our members are not exclusively lesbian. We prefer the company of women in our living situation and we want all of the women in the community to feel comfortable and safe. We started with seven people who thought it was a good idea — now we have 39 members ranging in age from 51 to 78. Just in the last two months we have had 37 inquiries, and we have a waiting list of women who'd like to be part of WINC.

My friend Anneke Deutsch was really the initiator of WINC. She had read about cohousing, and heard the US architect Charles Durrett speak about it at a conference. Charles's book *The Senior Cohousing Handbook* has really become the template for how we've developed our community.

We are following the suggested plan of three study groups. The first is "Ageing Well in Community" — we have run this group study several times as new members joined. The second is "Participatory Design", through which we have recently completed our masterplan. The third is "Policy": developing the policies that we will live by as a group of residents. This one hasn't been done as yet; we will complete it together when we know who will actually live in the community.

Originally we were hoping to build our community in Daylesford. We thought we had a site, and we were working with a developer, but after Covid the market price had gone up by $1 million, and we were priced out. Members agreed that a really important element was to have a train close by, so we found land in Castlemaine within 2.5 km of the train and the centre of town — it's beautiful, and we settled on that in March.

Clearly, finding land has been challenging! And of course the costs of housing have been going berserk, just as we are trying to plan our build. Many of our members are older women with very few resources, and getting funding has been really challenging too, as most banks simply won't lend to older women.

Ideally we would have found a developer to buy the land, develop the site, and then sell the houses off the plan to us, but that hasn't happened. In the end we created a company to raise the $2 million we needed to buy the land, and $250,000 to get the planning permits; we sourced this money from some of the members who could afford to make the investment. The creation of the company means that we can sell it on to a developer and get our money back, and then the developer can build the houses and sell those off the plan to our members … at least that's the plan.

WINC draft site map

WINC members pay a membership fee of around $150/year ($100/year concession). Members who are going to be owners have also paid 1% of their annual income to a maximum of $400 as a one-off organising fund, and a development levy of $1,900. Ongoing costs will be membership plus Owners Corporation fees, when the homes are purchased.

WINC has created the master site plan, engaged a civil engineer and town planner, and set up a development management team who are helping us with costing, and with finding a developer to build the community. One option is to engage a community housing provider, as we will have four houses within the community for social housing.

We are still trying to figure out a purchase option for the group we call the "middle women". These are the ones who have about half of what they need to buy a home. For example, someone who has $180,000 has too much to qualify for social housing but too little to actually house themselves. At the moment they may be paying half their income in rent. We want to have six or seven homes for this group, but we haven't quite worked out how to fund purchase options for them yet. The remaining 22 homes will be sold at roughly market price. While the prices are not yet confirmed, we are looking at a 50 m^2 one-bedroom home costing around $450,000; a 65 m^2 one-bedroom home for around $550,000; and an 80 m^2 two-bedroom home for around $650,000. Of course, these prices may well go up, but we're doing our best to keep them down. The prices also include shares in the common property in the community.

We are designing for interaction and community, sustainability and accessibility. For sustainability we are aiming for passive house standards, or a minimum 8 star energy performance. We also aim to meet universal accessibility standards, so that residents and visitors who are using a walker or wheelchair have complete access to their home, the common areas, and the paths around the community.

On our Castlemaine site there is already a 4-bedroom home that we will transform into two guest rooms with ensuites for visitors, and a common laundry, craft room and library/yoga/quiet room to foster informal connections. There will be a separate common house building with a communal kitchen, dining area and lounge, and we will design that so it can be opened up for large parties or events like a film night. Each home's kitchen will be on the small side, so the communal kitchen may also be used for making jam or entertaining friends who come over for smaller parties.

Once built, the ownership will operate as a strata title development. Many of the women want to be able to pass their assets on to their family, and strata is the most well-understood form of ownership. It is a reasonably straightforward form of contract and gives owners a good balance of rights and responsibilities. We work on consensus and strata title was the decision of the group.

I think if you are thinking about cohousing you need to take the time to get know the people who are likely to be your neighbours. We invite women to explore the process by coming to meetings and gatherings of different kinds to work out if it is for them. If they like it, then after a few months they can join. It's really a matter of getting to know people and working out who you are happy to spend the rest of your life with. We work hard to build community before we all live together. We have had members who joined and left and that's fine. We have some women who want to be nearby but not live in the community — we call them "periWINCles" because they'd like to stay on the perimeter of our community. We also have around 50 "Friends of WINC", who support what we do but don't necessarily want to live with us and that's okay, they are part of our broader community.

In our research we have found that the best size for a cohousing community is 25–30 homes. If the community is small, for example, around 6–8 homes, then you really need to get along very well with everyone. A community with 25–30 homes gives you scope to have a few really good friends in the community, a broader circle of friends, and then a broad range of acquaintances.

Nightingale

Nightingale aims to deliver financially, environmentally and socially sustainable buildings that connect residents with the community. They are currently active in Melbourne, regional Victoria, Adelaide and Sydney, and have thousands of people registered for their projects.

Nightingale Housing is a not-for-profit organisation that keeps costs low by eliminating what's not needed: there are no display suites (prospective buyers can tour existing, completed projects), no real estate agents, no individual laundries, no second bathrooms and no big basement carparks.

Traditional property development is all about creating profit for shareholders. In contrast, the Nightingale approach is to deliver housing at cost, and then to take any residual revenue from a project and put it back towards their mission of delivering environmentally, socially and financially sustainable housing. To maintain their not-for-profit status, they ensure any residual revenue (which might otherwise be considered 'profit') is used to further the purpose of the organisation, not for the benefit of individual shareholders as is the case in commercial property development.

Other Nightingale design principles include achieving a Nationwide House Energy Rating Scheme (NatHERS) of at least 7.6 stars, and powering buildings with a mix of solar power and 100% certified Green Power. Buildings also include shared rooftop gardens, laundries and dining areas. Prospective buyers register their details with Nightingale, and are notified when a project becomes available in their chosen area. Next, there are two information sessions that detail the project, the location, the design response, the team, and what makes a Nightingale community great. At this point, prospective buyers receive floor plans and indicative price ranges and can choose to enter the ballot.

If drawn in the ballot, buyers have 10 days to pay a commitment fee ($10,000 at time of writing) to secure the apartment. Contracts are then signed, and a 10% deposit is payable. The process is not for the impatient: the expected time frame from notification to moving is two to three years.

Nightingale believes that the residential property industry can and must do more to address housing inequality and insecurity. As such, they aim to pre-allocate up to 20% of each project to community housing providers, who give affordable, long term leases to vulnerable members of the community.

Through priority balloting, Nightingale also allocates 20% of available apartments in each building to key community contributors (e.g. teachers, nurses, social workers); individuals with a disability, carers, single women 55 and over, and Aboriginal and Torres Strait Islander Australians.

Nightingale Village, for example, is a collection of six neighbouring buildings, each designed by a different award-winning architect using the social, environmental and financial sustainability principles of the Nightingale model. These principles are embedded in every building, and across the village. The precinct is entirely fossil fuel-free. Across 203 homes, there are just 20 car spaces for share cars. And 20% of the project is made available to those most in need via community housing providers, Housing Choices Australia and women's property initiatives. In 2023, Nightingale Village won the prestigious Dimity Reed Melbourne Prize for its contribution to the city.

Mary* @ Nightingale

Downsizing is something you are best to do early. It's very liberating!

Downsizing was a process over many years for me. When my husband was alive we lived in a big old house on 12 acres in Queensland. Sadly he passed away when we were both 50, and with four kids I simply couldn't manage the house and land. So the kids and I moved to a smaller home in Noosa: still 4 bedrooms, but easier to maintain. Over the years, the kids moved out … a few of them moved to Melbourne, so I rented a townhouse close to them.

One of my sons is an architect, and he told me what Nightingale were doing. It had enormous appeal for me: it was an opportunity to put my money where my mouth is. Nightingale is an environmentally aware, carbon neutral building, and it seemed like the perfect opportunity to live that reality instead of just talking about it. So that downsizing decision was quite easy. It was also perfect timing, as I was ready to put down roots in Melbourne.

When I first investigated Nightingale, all of the apartments had already been allocated in the ballot. But two people had a change of circumstances, so I put my name down for the ballot for one of those and got my apartment! It is a one-bedroom, 60 m², tiny little space — but really well designed. I had never lived in an architect-designed home before, but I can see now why you would want to. It's a very high quality small space with beautiful finishes; it was so nice to move somewhere that I didn't have to renovate. The buildings are designed to be energy efficient, with flow-through air to keep the apartments cool in summer. I have a single hydronic heater for winter — there's no other heating, but on a 2-degree morning in Melbourne it's a lovely 20 degrees in my apartment. All of the windows are double glazed and the walls are insulated, so there's no air conditioning: it doesn't require a lot of extra input in terms of heating and cooling, it just works. My electricity costs are really low and there is no gas. I think my last power bill was about $50, but to be honest I don't pay too much attention these days, because I just don't have any, "Oh my goodness!" moments.

I'm in Nightingale 1, which is the smallest of the Nightingale buildings in Brunswick, Melbourne. It's close to Sydney Road, trams are super close and the train is just a three-minute walk away. I don't have a car any more, I use a bike and public transport, that's one of the ways Nightingale is planned. I have access to a car if I need it — there are go-get cars right outside the door, and I can borrow one of my kids' cars. Brunswick is so multicultural too, it's Melbourne living at its best: great coffee, great Lebanese food, great Japanese, an inner city hum, it's very alive.

I'm a good sharer, for me it's easy. I was a bit of a hippie when I was younger so sharing the laundry and other spaces is fine. I know all the people in my building, when I go to the laundry I normally bump into someone and have a chat, it's a nice little community of like-minded people. If I needed anything

I know I could ask one of my neighbours. But not having an outside space of my own has been hard, not having a little garden, the connection with the outside. I'm lucky to work in regional areas and that gives me a shot of nature — connection to the land, the sky, trees — but you have to get yourself out a bit more rather than sitting on the front verandah.

Nightingale 1

It's been interesting to see the reaction of friends and acquaintances my age: I can sense them thinking, "I couldn't live here". I think they have the usual expectations — the big house, the shed, the garden, the da-de-da … If our society and planet are going to survive we have to make changes, like downsizing. It's so nice to have a really low maintenance home with low energy costs, and hopefully be contributing to a better world. Our generation expected a house and a block of land, but my kids and their friends come in and go, "Wow, this is lovely!"

But, oh my God, downsizing all my stuff is still a challenge, I have a storage unit in Queensland that's full: my husband made beautiful furniture and I can't bear to part with it, but I don't have the space and nor do my kids. I joke that it's the most expensive furniture in the world.

I had amazing parents who always stepped into the next phase of their life before they had to, they downsized steadily right into their 80's. I think they were great role models, they taught me to take the next step before you need to — think about the future, and what legacy you can leave behind — I am very grateful to my parents for that.

I think downsizing is something you are best to do early, before something forces you. It's very liberating! I can lock my apartment, switch off everything except the fridge, and walk away for two months knowing that everything is safe. We have to do this, it's in every newspaper every day — we are the generation that has to take the biggest jump from the expectations we grew up with to the reality of what we need to aim for now. Be fearless — that's my advice.

* Names and other identifying factors have been changed at "Mary's" request.

New generation boarding houses

In NSW, the *Affordable Housing State Environmental Planning Policy 2009* (AHSEPP) brought in "new generation boarding house" provisions. The objective of the changes was to provide a consistent planning regime for affordable rental housing, provide incentives for more affordable housing to be created, and mitigate the loss of affordable housing.

The **Croydon conversion** is one example. This development was undertaken by Common Equity, NSW's peak body for housing cooperatives, which oversees the function and operation of 32 housing cooperatives across NSW, managing over 500 properties.

It involved reconfiguring an existing single family home in Sydney's Inner West to become multiple dwellings: four studio units on the ground floor, two of which are fully wheelchair accessible. Upstairs can form a single self-contained tenancy, or two separate spaces. Because the home is in a heritage conservation zone, the front part of the house remains intact and preserves the look and feel of the property from the street.

Shared areas include open-plan living, kitchen and dining; a separate storeroom and laundry; covered patio; and gardens. In addition, the existing carport has been redesigned to suit meetings and other group activities. The new design aims to create opportunities for interaction between cooperative members while maintaining privacy. It was finalised in consultation with members of existing housing cooperatives, to ensure a practical, liveable outcome.

While not specifically designed for older people, the Croydon conversion shows how existing middle-ring housing stock can be retrofitted to provide collaborative housing that meets the needs of a wide range of people.

It offers residents secure tenure in a well-developed legal structure, with support from Common Equity as needed. Cooperative members also contribute several hours to running the co-op and maintaining the property.

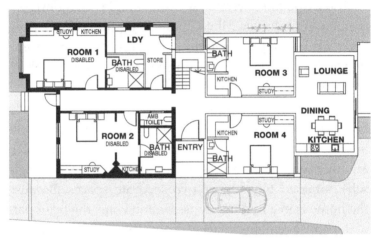

Source: Common Equity NSW and Prescott Architects

In Sydney's iconic beachside suburb of Bondi, **The Corner**, underwent a dramatic transformation in 2019, from its original eight 3-bedroom apartments, to 38 studio apartments, then known as the Bondi Treehouse. It was designed by Mark Shapiro Architects to increase the supply and diversity of affordable housing in the suburb. While their small size makes the studios affordable for the area (rents range from $700 to $800 a week), their designs are inspired by the luxury micro-apartments popping up in major cities around the world.

Source: Mark Shapiro Architects

Apartments are connected by wide corridors and vertical voids that bring greenery and airflow throughout the building. Low energy design features including thermal mass, shade screens and double glazing keep both private and shared spaces comfortable with minimal energy use.

Common outdoor spaces include an external shower, surf-board storage and a community garden; inside, there are multiple shared work and meeting spaces and two commercial tenancies, which are home to a clothing shop and a Japanese cafe. The building is under the care of an on-site manager.

Collaborative housing as part of a bigger development

Jasmine Grove is a small collaborative housing neighbourhood for women within a retirement village, IRT Kanahooka. IRT (originally known as Illawarra Retirement Trust) is a community-owned organisation founded in 1969 to offer better housing and care options for seniors.

Jasmine Grove has been designed specifically to encourage sharing of resources, spaces and everyday activities, allowing a more affordable, sustainable and enjoyable way of living for women over 55 living on their own.

The collaborative housing neighbourhood consists of eight 1-bedroom self-contained villas, each with its own kitchen and laundry, but sharing larger community spaces: a large community kitchen, dining room for eight people, community lounge, outdoor barbeque area, gardens, green spaces and storage.

Prices at Jasmine Grove range from $199,000 to $366,000 depending on which payment option you choose.

TABLE 9: Summary of IRT Jasmine Grove payment options

	Pay as you go	Departure fee	Pay upfront
Purchase price	$199,000	$260,000	$366,000
Recurrent fee	$127.58/ week	$127.58/ week	$127.58/ week
Contribution instalments	$230.00/ week	$0/week	$0/week
Exit entitlement after 6 years	$192,000	$182,000	$366,000

9

RETIREMENT COMMUNITIES

There are so many different types of retirement communities across Australia that the choices can seem overwhelming. Just like people, retirement communities come in all different shapes and sizes. Some are designed for people who need affordable housing; some appeal to people who wish to downsize their house and upsize their social life; while others are there to meet the needs of people who require care and support. Finding the community that you want to be a part of involves research. You'll need to look at the accommodation and community facilities, and the lifestyle the residents enjoy: the activities they are enjoying, the domestic help or care services available should you need it, and of course the legal and financial arrangements that apply.

If the whole thing is a bit of mystery to you, you are in the right place. We are going to talk you through the various types of retirement communities: how to choose one that suits you, contracts and costs and the various ways to fund your retirement lifestyle. We also share real-life stories and case studies to give you an insight into the experiences others have had and the lessons they have learnt.

In our experience, the biggest regret people have when moving to a retirement community is that they didn't do it sooner, so we aim to demystify it for you. We want you to become informed and take control of your future.

Why move to a retirement community?

Different people have very different ideas of what living in a retirement community is all about. Some picture very old people sitting around waiting for the inevitable, while others see a vibrant community of active people who are so busy they hardly have time to take part in all the activities. The fact is that retirement communities, like people, come in all different shapes and sizes … and what one person doesn't like may be another's utopia.

There is no doubt that the home environment is a major influence on the happiness of retirees, since their lifestyle tends to centre on activities in and around the home. In a 2018 survey of almost 20,000 retirement village residents across 529 villages, 15% said that their happiness levels had decreased, while 85% reported that their happiness levels were the same or greater since they moved to the village, with 26% reporting a significant increase in their level of happiness.

While people's motivations for moving to a retirement community vary, when you talk to enough people, you see that most fall into two categories. One is those who are moving for lifestyle, because they want the companionship of like-minded people, to participate in activities, a home they can "lock and leave" and more time for fun. The other is those people who are moving to a retirement community because they don't want to (or can't) maintain their current home, it is not safe, or similar reasons. They may fancy the security of living in a community and the company of like-minded people, and they may need some support and perhaps care to remain living independently.

In either case, moving beats the alternative of staying in the old home out of a fierce sense of independence, or a sense of obligation to grown-up children, if the cost is struggling to maintain that home and being socially isolated in it. Moving to a retirement community gives people greater security and freedom of choice. The facilities and gardens are maintained, in many cases meals and laundry (and care) can be provided, and residents can take part in activities of their choosing yet be alone when the mood takes them. That to us is true independence — being master of your own destiny and still part of a community.

Retirement communities provide their residents with wonderful facilities, such as pickle ball courts, bowling greens, cinemas, club houses, gymnasiums, cafes, swimming pools and more. Best of all, you are likely to live in a close-knit community of people with whom you can share the good times (and the not-so-good ones too). It makes good sense to consider a move to a retirement community sooner rather than later, when you can get the most out of it. Many of the retirement communities we have visited are ideally suited to people who are young, fit and healthy. They would be a perfect place to semi-retire, and a number of the residents who live there have done exactly that, working two or three days a week and enjoying the rest of the week playing golf and socialising.

While it may be hard to tell the difference between a retirement village and a land lease community, those differences are important. We will look at the different legal and financial arrangements that apply to each in a later chapter.

If you are considering moving to a retirement community, these are the factors that may swing your decision towards making the move:

1. **Maintaining a house.** You may be getting tired of mowing, painting, gardening and fishing leaves out of a pool that is rarely used — or paying for someone else to tend to these things. You may also be sick of attending to what can seem like a constant influx of bills such as rates and insurance. No more ladders for you — let someone else do the work!

2. **Social life.** Your children may be scattered throughout the country and while you are perfectly capable of getting involved in groups and clubs, you don't seem to be able to find the energy to make it happen. Similarly, you would love the opportunity for some travel but you don't want to go alone. As a result, you find yourself spending more and more time in front of the television set and realise you are in danger of vegetating.

3. **Sport.** You love to swim, walk, play bowls, golf, tennis, boating, cards or all of these things. A villa on the ninth hole or with direct access to the marina may be just the place for you.

4. **Health.** Maybe you or a friend have had a health scare and you realise it would be comforting for you to have help close by. A village with care and support can be a great alternative to one member of a couple living in care on their own.

If you can recognise yourself in one or more of the above situations, a retirement community may be a good option.

Leslie @ Henry Kendall Gardens

I would do it all again. It's freedom. I don't have a house around my neck.

I'm not really a procrastinator, I started thinking about downsizing about six months before I moved into the village. I shopped around for several weeks, I looked at strata title developments, it was actually my children — who live overseas — who suggested I look at a retirement village, so I looked at a few.

This village appealed to me because it is well-established, and it is very safe. My neighbours are terrific, it is great to be in a community of like-minded people, there's no wild parties, or inconsiderate people playing loud music all the time. You don't necessarily know everyone, or socialise with everyone, but people will always smile and wave. When I first came to the village, I was very pleasantly surprised — I wanted to move in straight away, but it took a little bit of time to sell my home.

Leslie in her home at Henry Kendall Gardens

Selling my home wasn't hard; the number of maintenance jobs seemed to be growing and the number that I could do myself was reducing. The hard part was getting rid of some of my furniture. I kept enough to fill my apartment: the rest I gave away to friends or charities and some I sold to a broker. My

real estate agent was a wonderful resource in identifying how to sell and donate the things I no longer
needed. While it was tough, at the end I felt a wonderful freedom from things that I no longer need
or use.

I am over the moon that I made the decision to
downsize, and in the hard times I thought about
what my life was going to be like when I got here.
It's freedom. I don't have a house around my neck. I
don't need to look after all that furniture, gardens —
I have realised that big houses tie you down, we can
be healthier and happier in a small house with less
responsibility.

I have two bedrooms and two bathrooms: one for
visitors so my kids (or grandkids) can come and stay
quite comfortably. I have never been bored; there is
so much to do and I haven't lost my social connections. I still go to my quilting group and I work part
time at a radio station as a volunteer.

Downsizing frees up your money and frees up
your time. I did my sums on living here, it's $50
per month more to live in the village. But in my old
house the hot water service blew not long before I
sold and it cost me $1200, the same thing happened
within three months of me moving in and they replaced it straight away with no cost and no hassle.
The payment options were fantastic — I think there
is something for everyone — I paid my management
fee upfront, which was an extra 18% on the purchase
price, my contract still allows me to get any capital
gain but gives me the security of knowing exactly

how much I will pay and it's less than if you pay at the end.

Even though I freed up a little bit of money from selling my home, my pension hasn't changed, and my utilities are definitely cheaper because I only pay electricity and gas in the village. The bus is great — it cuts down on needing to use the car and there are lots of visiting services, like doctors, which are very convenient.

I think anyone thinking about downsizing should look around, look at different options like apartments and units, then look at the facilities and amenities you can get in a village compared with the price. Get legal advice to run through the contract — my lawyer helped me understand it. Peace of mind is worth more than anything else.

Field guide to community types

There are many terms used by retirement communities, from traditional terms like "over 55's" and "retirement village", to fancy terms like "gated community", "lifestyle resort", "care community". While this range of names may make it appear that there are too many different legal and financial arrangements to compare, in reality, most retirement communities fall into one of two groups, which we will refer to as "retirement villages" and "land lease communities".

Retirement villages operate under the relevant state or territory legislation, typically the *Retirement Villages Act*.

The legislation generally:

- defines a retirement village
- sets a minimum age for living in one (typically 55)
- sets out what legal documents (including disclosures) must be provided to residents by the village operator
- regulates some — not all — financial arrangements, such as under what circumstances the operator must buy back the unit if it remains unsold and for how long after leaving the village you will be responsible for on-going charges
- provides a framework for resolving disputes.

Retirement villages commonly feature emergency call bells, and accommodation may be freestanding houses, duplexes or apartments.

While people must be over 55 to live in a retirement village, the average age at which people move is 75, and the average age of current residents is 81, according to the Property Council 2022 Census. Of course, averages can be misleading: an average age of 81 could mean half the people living in retirement villages were 90 and half were 72, or that half were 65 and the other half were 97, or that ages were spread from 61 to 105. The point is that retirement villages are definitely not *only* for people who are retired and over the age of 70; there is a growing cohort of young, fit, active retirees choosing to live in retirement communities. In some cases they are still working — and lobbying for the community not to have the word "retirement" in its name!

A range of modern retirement communities are going up to cater for people who want to downsize close to where they currently live. Because they are in areas that are close to shops, transport, sporting venues and entertainment precincts, many of these are vertical communities with luxury amenities to rival a six-star resort, or a cruise ship.

A good example is **Ardency Kennedy Place**, where the first residents are just moving in. Ardency is Keyton Group's collection of luxury retirement communities, of which there are three in NSW; Kennedy Place will be the first to open in Victoria.

Ardency Kennedy Place is located on the site of the former Channel 9 studios in Bendigo Street, Richmond, and named after the former "King of Australian Television", Graham Kennedy. Being in the heart of Richmond, there is easy access to Swan Street, Bridge Road, the Yarra River, and it is just a short tram ride to Melbourne CBD.

The precinct incorporates heritage listed buildings, cafés, the Richmond Community Learning Centre, 31 Gramercy Terraces residential homes and a proposed residential aged care home. The village consists of 116 luxury apartments designed by award winning architects Bates Smart and offers residents world class amenities including a concierge, resident lounge with fireplace, billiards table and baby grand piano, 30-seat cinema, a wellness Centre with indoor heated swimming pool, gym, yoga studio, rooftop terrace with city views and more.

Apartment prices start from $990,000 for a two-bedroom residence and $1,220,000 for a three-bedroom residence; at the time of writing all of the one-bedroom apartments are sold out. Penthouses are priced from $1,550,000.00 to $3,380,000.00.

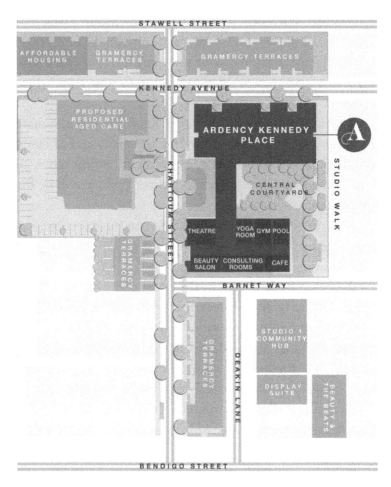

Ardency Kennedy Place Precinct Map

In **land lease communities (LLCs)**, technically, all the homes are removable, and the residents lease the land — so the current terminology makes sense. LLCs rarely offer emergency call bells, and are often larger communities, both physically — because buildings are required to be demountable, each stands alone — and in numbers: it is common to have 300+ homes. They are ideally suited to the current trend for "tiny homes" too.

Of course there is always the exception to the rule: Gem-Life, an LLC operator with communities across Victoria, New South Wales and Queensland has plans to build the first "vertical land lease community" on the Gold Coast — and yes, the homes will still be able to be removed!

LLCs grew out of caravan parks, and while, like retirement villages, they operate under state or territory legislation, it is normally the same legislation that governs caravan parks. This may be via specific acts, such as the *Residential (Land Lease) Communities Act (NSW)*, as part of each state's residential tenancies act, or under a combination of acts.

Caravan parks are often thought of as a place to visit on your way around Australia — on the "grey nomad trail" — many LLCs cater exclusively to retirees, but there are a few that cater to both tourists and permanent residents. The key difference here is that caravan park residents will have a rental agreement, while the LLC (designed as over-55's communities through a restriction in their community rules) are much more likely to be leasehold arrangements.

A good example of a land lease community that is co-located with a holiday park is Ingenia Lifestyle Lake Conjola. There is a separate entrance for the lifestyle community residents, who have paid between $300,000 and

$635,000 dollars for their homes, and pay $205/week in site fees. The tourist park has 368 sites, a private boat ramp, café, waterslide and water park, tennis courts, a putt-putt course, barbeque areas, and a children's playground. In peak season there can be 1,250 visitors, which means the lifestyle community residents can make new friends, have old friends (or family) come to stay or retreat to the relative peace and quiet of their community. Of course, the benefit of having all of the facilities of the tourist park is that the lifestyle community residents can use them year-round.

Ingenia Lifestyle Lake Conjola shares the holiday park facilities, such as the water park and BBQ area, which is ideal when family visit

Andrew @ The Landings

We've seen the good and bad sides of retirement villages.

I hadn't been thinking about downsizing. I was working overseas, but my wife was struggling with a big house and property that she couldn't maintain on her own. She visited the village because we had friends living there. We only lived 1 km down the road — ironically, when I saw it being built years earlier, I thought, "Who'd want to live there?!"

It only took us six months from the day we decided to downsize to the day we moved in. Getting rid of goods and chattels my son said to me, "Dad, you've had the utility out of it, let it go". I was surprised that my three brothers were quite negative: they said to me, "Are you mad? Retirement villages are for old people."

When we moved into the village in 2007, we had friends who lived there, and several ex-service people also. I felt that the village had a commitment to ex-service people, and it was quite an inducement that we would get $30,000 off the list price in recognition of service.

Before my wife and I signed the contract, we were told to get legal advice — which we did. We used a reputable company, every clause was vetted by the lawyer, and they alerted us to issues of concern. The only significant one they found was that in the event the dwelling wasn't sold after we moved out, the buyback period would only begin after seven years!

We and almost every resident got legal advice before we moved in — and understood our entitlements and obligations. We were fortunate that our contracts were leasehold, which meant that remediation of the building defects was very clearly the operator's responsibility.

Andrew at the Landings

The problem, I think, is that not many lawyers understand the retirement village industry. They look at it like a normal contract, expecting it to be enforceable, but people in their twilight years, many of whom are widows, don't have the knowhow, funds or energy to battle with big companies, they need good reliable advice to avoid stress.

The prime mover in the development of the village was the Royal Australian Airforce Association (RAAFA), who sold their share in 2009 to their partner Sakkara. RAAFA didn't really have anything to do with running the village.

It became increasingly apparent, by 2008, that there were significant building defects in both the communal buildings and the dwellings. It was everything — from painting to tiling, waterproofing of showers and roofs, even the fire-proofing. There were so many defects it was unbelievable.

The issues we had were very well publicised. From memory, we had 20 visits to tribunals (not all were successful, but we were more successful than not), and got an estimated $2m of defective building works fixed. In 2008, the operator was already embroiled in a claim with its insurer for defective building works. We thought that commencing action at the tribunal would assist the operator by proving to the insurer that the building defects were substantial and real, and placing the operator under a further obligation to get them remediated. But in the end, it just soured the relationship between residents and the operator.

When we went to tribunal none of us used our own lawyers — as a group, we engaged a lawyer who specialised in this area. My advice to anyone looking at moving into a village would be to obtain advice from someone who truly understands and has experience in the retirement village industry. Don't go to just any lawyer, make sure they know the industry. If you can go to forums at the village you plan to enter, where you can speak to residents, then that is a real advantage. Now, with my experience of retirement village life, I wouldn't move in if I couldn't gain real resident feedback. Recourse through tribunals or government is not a solution, because they simply have no hands-on knowledge — it is better to do your own homework.

It took from 2008, when the issues of the building defects were first noted, until 2012 to get the majority of defects dealt with. Some are still evident. The longest of the cases took us two years and cost residents $140,000.

But this story does have a happy ending. We are fortunate now that we are seeing the other side of the coin: our village was sold to LDK Healthcare in February 2019 and we couldn't be happier.

Carefree or cared for?

What will happen if you need care? This is a question you should consider when you are looking at any accommodation you plan on downsizing into. After all, the ability to get care in your new home may be the difference between being able to stay or needing to move again.

Many granny flats and homes in retirement communities are built with "care infrastructure". It is more common in buildings from the mid-2010s onwards.

This infrastructure may not be obvious but if you ever need it you will see the features in a whole new light. Some typical examples are wide doors and hallways — they look great and give a sense of space to the home, and they also make it simple to get around with a walker, sometimes even a wheelchair. Showers with no recess (and possibly dual entry points) look luxurious, make it easy to get in and out as there is no step, and are perfect if you need someone to assist you with showering.

Some key infrastructure is not even visible, for example, using tiles with a higher slip rating. Installing kitchen appliances as a "wall tower" means that ovens are at chest height and microwaves can be placed so hot foods are safe to handle. This is a feature you'll enjoy now, and get even more benefit from later in life.

Having anchor points and supports inside the walls for installing grab rails and weight bearing accessories is really important, though you cannot see them. Rails screwed into plaster won't save you if you fall. If the anchors are not already there, installing grab rails will involve removing the plaster, adding additional timber supports into the wall framing, replastering, repainting, and finally attaching the grab rails. This exercise is neither quick nor cheap but installing the supports in the original build is both. Then you can add the rails if and when you want to.

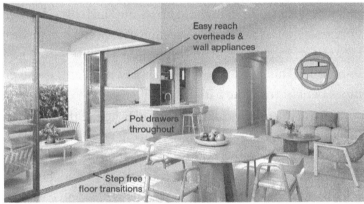

Easy reach overheads & wall appliances

Pot drawers throughout

Step free floor transitions

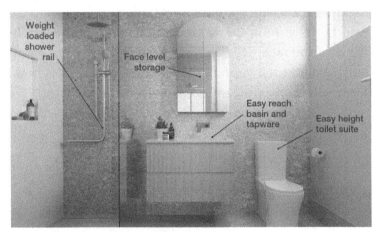

Weight loaded shower rail

Face level storage

Easy reach basin and tapware

Easy height toilet suite

Source: Ingenia Lifestyle Natura

Source: Ingenia Lifestyle Natura

Retirement communities, whether classed as retirement villages or LLCs, generally offer two types of accommodation: independent living and supported living.

While there may be an aged care facility located on the same site, the financial arrangements that apply there are completely different. Most people assume that residents of a co-located retirement community receive priority access to the aged care facility, or get a financial advantage in transferring to the aged care facility, but this is not normally true — only a handful of places have such models. So it is important to know how much care you can receive in your retirement community, under what circumstances you can be asked to leave, and whether or not your financial position will enable you to afford the care you want and need. If the retirement community tells you they have an arrangement that enables you to transfer into aged care with preferential treatment, make sure you look into it; if you want to go down that road your contract will need to have the agreement stated in it.

First, let's look at independent living in a retirement community, and then compare it with living in a serviced apartment or supported living community. We explore some of the new options that help you move from independent to supported living and/or aged care in the next chapter.

Independent living

Independent living in a retirement community differs little from living in your own home, though if you are still in a family-sized home, you will probably be downsizing. The major benefit is the ability to enjoy the community facilities without paying membership fees or having to travel to them. In a retirement village you also get freedom from maintenance chores — no heavy expenditure such as painting your house or replacing the guttering — but in an LLC you own the home so it will normally be up to you to maintain it inside and out.

Activities are typically centred around the social heart of the community — the leisure centre, clubhouse or recreation hall — where residents meet and there is a calendar of events. Depending on the community, residents may meet for a round of golf, a spot of fishing at the lake, a walk or bike ride along the paths and trails, a game of billiards, book club in the library, a few laps or a game of volleyball in the swimming pool, or some lawn bowls, tennis or the current sporting craze — pickleball. A word of warning: the competitions (and the trophies that go with them) can be very hotly contested!

A big plus is the companionship of like-minded people. This is particularly important if you lose your partner because, even though you have lost a major figure in your life, you have not lost the other friends around you. Thus, you still have a major emotional support base at a time in your life when you need it most, and your independence and contact with your friends is not suddenly taken from you. Remember, the latest research shows that your network of friends is a major indicator of how long and how happily you will live.

Another bonus is that in a retirement village the independent living units and apartments are likely to have an emergency call system. Some call emergency services, i.e., triple 000, some call on-site care, and others alert a list of people, often both family and emergency services.

Trish @ Uniting, Leichardt

Having assistance to keep me living independently for as long as possible is the greatest comfort.

I lived in Canberra and I wanted to move closer to my family in Sydney, so that was really my motivation. My health wasn't good at the time and I wanted to have a sense of having support around me without losing my independence.

I didn't really consider moving into an apartment, I was looking at independent living in a retirement village, I wanted to make a move that was future proof — you never know what the future holds. My daughter saw this village being built and told me about it, I saw a model early on and had some floorplans but I never actually saw my apartment until the day I moved in. My daughter and son-in-law kept an eye on the development and kept me up to date with what was happening to smooth my way forward.

It was about 18 months between expressing interest and moving in (Covid meant it was a bit longer than I first thought). It was actually an ideal amount of time, I wasn't rushed, I could make decisions and

I had time to get organised — I sold my apartment and took out some of my super to give me the funds to buy my apartment. The folk at Uniting offered me a huge amount of support during this time. On the day I moved in I came in the morning and my apartment faces east, the sun was streaming in and I felt at home straight away. It was just a feeling of contentment.

I'm not a sentimental person about physical things; people are what I care about most. Moving from Canberra meant I left my social networks behind, which was a bit daunting. I came here knowing nobody, but with my daughter a few streets away. I'm not an overly outgoing person, I didn't have any fears of being isolated, but I think some of my family thought I might bury myself in my unit. I definitely haven't done that.

Moving into a new village meant that all of the residents moved in at around the same time and in a short time a wonderful sense of community developed. People can be involved in the many activities or remain more private. There's a choir; book, gardening, and walking groups, as well as a dinner group that tries local restaurants once a week. The knitting group is very productive, and has made several hundred beanies for the "hats for the homeless" initiative — and now we are knitting a nativity scene to go into the foyer at Christmas.

Because public transport is so convenient I am able to enjoy many activities outside of the village.

A friend and I regularly go to concerts, including at the Opera House and similar venues. My mobility is somewhat limited, so I applied for the government's Companion Card and this means we are able to enjoy these outings at a really reduced cost. Downsizing has opened up a whole new world to me: I was living in a bigger home, but I wasn't really able to get out and do too much.

Trish and her daughter Rose

I have no regrets about downsizing. It's wonderful to not be responsible for home maintenance — if a light bulb needs replacing I don't have to worry about it. I just contact the maintenance team and they fix it for me, it's a big relief.

If I was going to give someone advice about downsizing, I would say to explore the options but don't be fearful — you have to be able to live the life you want to live. Location is really important, access to shops, medical services and public transport. All of our futures are unknown, so making a plan that means you are protected and supported when things change is a good idea. Knowing that I have assistance to keep me living independently for as long as possible is the greatest comfort to me.

Supported living

A supported living unit is rather like a serviced apartment: it provides a higher level of assistance, generally through domestic services such as cleaning, laundry and changing linen, and cooking meals.

In some circumstances, the operator will deliver care through the Commonwealth Home Support Programme, your home care package, private carers or a combination of these. Increasing demand for care services from existing residents has pushed many operators into providing these services, but if the retirement community cannot organise this for you, you can make your own arrangements just as you would in your own home.

Traditional retirement communities that focus on lifestyle and activities want to attract residents who are sociable and physically active. These communities may require that you leave if your health deteriorates, as too many people unable to engage in social activities is not good for the other residents and makes it hard to sell units to active new residents.

Access to care is becoming a key consideration for people moving into retirement communities in their mid-70s, and is often a factor for those entering as a couple. A retirement community that can provide care services or that has an aged care facility located on-site is often a good solution where one member of a couple requires care but the other doesn't. Such arrangements can enable them to be close together, which would not be possible if the retirement community offered independent living only.

Ryman retirement villages incorporate independent living, serviced apartments, home care services and aged care facilities all on the one site, allowing residents to remain in the same village while meeting their care needs as they change over time. Ryman has eight villages already built, one under construction and five more planned across Victoria.

The deferred management fee (DMF) paid at exit reaches its top level after five years: 20% of your purchase price, with no capital gain or loss, no renovation costs, and no marketing or selling fees. People who transition from independent living to a serviced apartment are only charged the DMF on their first move.

In the serviced apartments there is a higher weekly service fee, which includes a daily chef-prepared meal, 24/7 nurse on call, and housekeeping. Many residents use their home care package to subsidise this fee.

People needing higher levels of care can choose to move into the aged care facility, which offers low care, high care, and specialist dementia care.

When a resident leaves a Ryman village, the company guarantees repayment of their original capital sum (less the DMF) within six months, or when the unit is sold — whichever comes first.

RetireAustralia has 29 communities in metropolitan, regional and coastal locations across Queensland, New South Wales and South Australia. Their philosophy is to create communities that support people to live independently in their own homes for as long as possible, ideally until end of life. To that end, they offer a continuum of care to support residents as their care needs change over time. RetireAustralia is also an approved home care provider; wherever possible they assist residents to access federally funded home care packages to help offset the cost of care services.

Glengara Care, on the New South Wales Central Coast, offers an alternative to residential aged care, located within Glengara Retirement Village. Here, care is under your control, couples stay together, small pets are welcome, and you live in the privacy of your own apartment. You can also come and go as you please while still receiving high levels of care.

To help residents manage their care costs at Glengara Care, RetireAustralia establishes a trust account in each resident's name with an independent body. This is called a care services account, and residents make regular contributions into this account which is drawn upon in line with their agreed care plan and when their costs of care exceed the value of their home care package, if they have one. The care services account is essentially a safety net to support residents to access high levels of care when they need it most. When a resident leaves Glengara Care, charges associated with the delivery of care cease immediately, and any funds in their care services account are refunded within 45 days.

RetireAustralia offers a single contract, with a DMF capped at 35% of your purchase price after three years. There is no capital gain or loss, or related selling costs, so you can calculate your exit entitlement at any time and know exactly what you will receive. There is a guaranteed buyback time of six months for NSW villages and 18 months for Queensland and South Australian villages. They also give you the ability to move to a different unit, or type of care accommodation, within their network and transfer the equity in your existing unit towards purchasing a different unit. Because RetireAustralia only charges one DMF, if you move to a different unit or care accommodation within their network your DMF calculation does not restart. This can be a great option if you wish to move interstate to be closer to family, or if your care needs are increasing and you want to stay within, or close to, your community.

Jim and Gina @ Glengara

We found the flexibility we needed.

After Jim's second heart attack, he and his wife Gina decided to move into RetireAustralia's Glengara Retirement Village on the NSW Central Coast, where they purchased a two-bedroom independent living villa for $650,000 in 2017.

Both in their late seventies at the time, Gina was worried about Jim's health and wanted him to stop doing so much maintenance around the house. Meanwhile, Jim wanted to ensure that Gina would be taken care of if something happened to him.

Eighteen months after they moved in, Gina had knee surgery so they enlisted support from the RetireAustralia home care team to assist Gina with personal care, house cleaning, preparing meals, laundry and linen. Gina's level 1 home care package contributed $750 to this a month and the couple contributed $1,050 a month from their own funds. Once Gina had recovered, they no longer needed assistance with personal care and meal preparation, but continued with house cleaning, laundry, and linen, which were covered by Gina's home care package.

They enjoyed three years in the village together before Jim passed away. During that time, they were both regulars at happy hour and mahjong, and Gina also went along to aqua aerobics, and book club. Gina continued to live independently in their villa for another two years before moving into a care apartment at Glengara Care after she was diagnosed with a heart condition in 2021. The ingoing contribution for a care apartment was $600,000. As Gina had been in their villa for five years, her deferred management fee had fully accrued, and she had $422,500 of equity (her exit entitlement) in her villa which she could use to help fund her new care apartment.

Following a care assessment with the Glengara Care team, Gina moved straight into her care apartment with an agreement in place to pay the ingoing contribution of $600,000 in instalments. A few months later, Gina's villa was sold and the equity of $422,500 was released and added to her care apartment as the first instalment. The second instalment of $177,500 was deferred.

When the time comes for Gina to vacate her care apartment and it is sold, the ingoing contribution of $600,000 will be returned. The second instalment of $177,500, which was deferred, will be deducted from the $600,000, leaving Gina with an exit entitlement of $422,500. She will pay no sales or marketing fees to sell her apartment and is guaranteed a buyback if it isn't sold within six months.

With meals, cleaning, laundry and linen, and case management included in the services at Glengara Care, the only support Gina needed to pay for when she first moved in was assistance with taking her medication four times a day. This was funded through her level 1 home care package and $410 per week from her care services account. Later on she was approved for a level 2 home care package, which reduced the contribution from her care services account to $262 per week.

Gina has continued to play mahjong with support, and she enjoys socialising with her friends at mealtime. As her health has continued to decline, her care and support has increased. Her family and the care team meet fortnightly to review and update her care plan. They have worked towards increasing her home care package: she now receives a level 4 package, which provides $4,870 a month towards her care. Gina is now receiving 9 hours and 15 minutes of care per week, which costs $4,400 a month and is funded by her home care package.

There are retirement communities that are purpose-built to deliver care and support from the time you move in. Sometimes it is hard to spot the difference between one of these and an aged care facility, as the apartments or units are often built to the same specifications: wide doorways to fit wheelchairs and lifting apparatus; bathrooms with handrails; and open shower areas that enable staff to assist with showering. Meals, domestic services and nursing services may be delivered to you as your care needs increase, or it may be a condition of entry that you already need some or all of these services to be provided.

Where it is a condition of entry that you require care, the care manager will generally assess your needs before you move in to ensure that they can provide the appropriate services. They will often coordinate the package of services for you and provide you with a price table to help you understand what the cost will be now and what you can expect if your care needs increase in the future. In many cases the care being provided will be through a government-funded home care package with the operator delivering any "top up" services themselves or through private contractors.

The key considerations if you are thinking about moving to one of these retirement communities are:

1. What are my care needs now? What are they likely to be over the next 10 years? At what point can the village no longer provide the care or services I require? Can I afford to stay in the village if my care needs increase significantly?

2. How do I feel about living with other people who have care needs that are likely to increase?

3. How will I fund my next move?

Odyssey Lifestyle Care Communities

Odyssey combines a retirement resort with 24/7 care. There are studio, 1, 2 and 3 bedroom apartments across their three buildings, all located at Robina on the Gold Coast. The village offers a fully licenced à la carte restaurant, activities centre, piano room, café, large al fresco area, gym, and library.

Care is delivered by a team of registered nurses, enrolled nurses, and personal carers, with at least one registered nurse on-site 24/7, and there are also lifestyle coordinators organising activities seven days per week.

The purchase price of apartments ranges from $620,000 to $990,000.

Residents pay $345 per week (fixed for life) which includes emergency nurse call, rates, building insurance, water, daily continental breakfast and high tea, concierge services, activities, amenities, security systems, bus services and periodic care consultations.

Chef-prepared meals are provided at cost — from $8 for a light meal to $14.50 for a three-course à la carte meal. Care is also provided at cost, with most residents using their home care package funding to pay towards these expenses.

There are three options for exit fee options (DMFs), which range from 22.5% to 37.5% of the purchase price.

While it is not compulsory that you need care to move into Odyssey, around 85% of the residents are receiving at least some care and support to continue living independently.

The attraction of such an offering includes that couples can stay together, residents and visitors can bring their pets, grandkids can have sleep-overs and you have the dignity and privacy of an apartment where you can do as much or as little as you want to do for yourself, with care and support for the rest.

Jan @ Odyssey, Robina

I found my tribe here. You have to make the effort; if you don't, you can be lonely for the rest of your life.

There are some people that think they will never leave home: "Carry me out in a box", they say, But that wasn't me, I have a very different mind-set. My husband and I downsized some years ago, we left our big home in Sydney and moved to a retirement village on the Central Coast. At the time I remember people saying to my husband, "You're too young to move to a retirement village" — he was in his 80's. We had extremely busy lives. I was involved with Probus, a couple of book clubs, a film appreciation group and my husband was involved in gliding (it was something he had always enjoyed).

After we had been in the village for about nine years our health was not great, and my husband was 12 years older than me. We dreaded the idea of moving to a nursing home, but we knew we couldn't stay where we were either. This village has 24/7 nurses, personal carers and a doctor 3–4 days a week. My problem was that I kept falling over; my husband couldn't get me up so he had to call the ambulance — it was embarrassing and upsetting (once it happened three times in a weekend). I really was wondering why I should go on.

Our daughter-in-law told us about Odyssey on the Gold Coast. Of course, our first thought was that we weren't keen to move to Queensland: it's too damn hot, and we would literally be leaving everything behind — our friends, my daughter, all of our social groups — everything.

Our son asked his sister to fly up and have a look, so she did. When she got back, she gave us a presentation — it ticked all of our boxes, so we moved. Sadly, we were only here for seven weeks when my husband passed. He was 94, and we'd been married for 60 great years: I like to think that we both chose well.

I really wasn't part of the community here for the first three months. My son nagged me to get involved so I went down to have lunch in the restaurant: lunch is served every day. It took me about three months of eating lunch and chatting (or not) to different people before I found my tribe here — we love chatting about books and politics and movies — but you have to make the effort; if you don't, you can be lonely for the rest of your life. That's definitely been my biggest challenge: making a new network of friends. I made new friends when I moved from Sydney to the Central Coast, and then again here. Being on the Gold Coast, I have friends from Sydney who come over for lunch or coffee if they are up this way, which is lovely.

Jan

Everyone here is so lovely. They treat everyone with

kindness and respect, and they really want to know how you are doing. The staff here are very well cared for, and in turn so are we. If something goes wrong — anything at all — I just press a button and they come to help me, which is a great comfort to me and to my children. From the CEO to the person serving me lunch today who said, "Jan, I hope you really enjoy your meal", they all know me. It might seem like a little thing that the person who serves your lunch knows who you are and knows what you like, but it's actually a big thing, It makes you feel as though you are within a family. That's been my biggest surprise — how hard it is to find a care community, and the fact that they all really do care here.

I'm 85 and absolutely need support to stay independent, but I don't want to feel like I'm old. It's like in that movie, Dirty Dancing, "Don't put baby in the corner". We all have thoughts, ideas, and many of us still have wonderful memories; we don't want to be put in a corner just because we are older.

It's a hard thing to do, but I say, "Do it!". You don't want to get to the point where you are forced to move, or move to somewhere you don't want to. Make the decision yours. Make sure you move before you "have to".

10

RETIREMENT COMMUNITY COSTS

Next let's examine the costs of living in a retirement community. Some of the most important questions are:

- What are you getting for the price you pay?
- What will it cost you each week or month?
- How much will you get back after you move out (and how soon)?

It's important to be aware that any costs associated with providing you with care or other services are normally in addition to the retirement community's fees and charges.

Retirement village disclosures

Retirement villages must give you a disclosure statement before you sign your contract. The minimum time period you have to consider the information before you can enter into a contract — often 14–21 days — is set by state-based legislation. In many cases the operator will give you a contract to review at the same time.

The village disclosure document outlines the nature of your contract and the key financial information. It includes the ingoing prices and any extra costs such as car parking, storage, contract preparation fees or stamp duty. Then there's the ongoing fees and their frequency — weekly, fortnightly or monthly. Finally, the exit entitlement calculations: whether a Deferred Management Fee (DMF) applies, if so how it is calculated, what your share will be of capital gain or capital loss, whether you will be responsible for reinstating or renovating your home after you leave, and how much you will need to pay for selling costs such as marketing, advertising, sales fees and legal fees. The disclosure document will typically provide a projection of your exit entitlement over a period of years, based on the operator's exit fee accumulation time frame or a set range of, say, 1, 2, 5 and 10 years.

The village disclosure document can also provide you with other important information, such as any debt or other encumbrances over the land that take priority over the rights of residents, whether or not the village has plans to expand or redevelop, the current weekly or monthly maintenance fee and any costs not included in that, which village fees will continue after your departure and for how long, and the time frame of any buyback.

Some operators will go above and beyond the mandatory disclosure documents and provide you with a Village Guru report. Village Guru is a software program that Rachel designed a couple of years ago. It produces a report that is far easier to understand than the disclosure documents, giving you details of the village costs grouped as ingoing, ongoing and outgoing, plus an estimate of your age pension and rent assistance entitlements, and your home care package fees and funding. The Village Guru report can show you up to three options side by side, which is ideal if you are comparing different properties or payment options in a village, or if you want to compare one village with another or against your current home.

Don't estimate

Because it's all quite complex people often try to estimate the costs, using simplifications or "rules of thumb" to compare their options. They say things like, "Well this unit is $500,000 and that one is $600,000, so this one is cheaper," or "That one has an exit fee of 30% and this one is 35% so that one is more affordable". But retirement community agreements are unlike other property transactions. Yes, the price or the DMF percentage may be less on one compared with another, but that doesn't mean that it is the cheapest or best value for money; you have to look at the whole transaction.

Let's now break the costs down into those three types: ingoing, ongoing and outgoing.

- **Ingoing** — all of the costs associated with entry to the community. The biggest, of course, is normally your purchase price
- **Ongoing** — costs associated with living in the community, combined with your own personal living expenses
- **Outgoing** — exit costs.

Ingoing costs

This is the price you pay to gain possession of your new home. The main part is your purchase price: the cost of the lease, licence or title for your home, depending on your contract type. There may also be buying costs, such as stamp duty and contract preparation fees. Stamp duty will depend on the type of ownership for your unit, and the exact calculation varies from state to state. Contract preparation fees vary from one village to another, but are often between $1,000 and $2,000.

Where you have bought off the plan, or paid a fee to put a hold on a house or unit or be part of a waiting list, the associated fees are normally taken into consideration in the purchase price. For example, if you paid a holding deposit of $5,000 and the purchase price was $350,000, you would pay the balance of $345,000 on settlement. In some cases, you pay a holding deposit for the initial expression of interest, then between 10% and 50% of the purchase price when you enter the contract to buy, and the balance when you take possession of the unit.

A number of the big operators offer a "move-in guarantee" — this basically extends the contract settling-in period set by the legislation, which may be as little as three days, up to as much as six months (in some cases). Essentially, if you move into a retirement community with a move-in guarantee and you decide that it's not for you within the time frame specified then you will get back your purchase price: there won't be an exit fee. But you may be charged a market price rent for the time that you have lived there.

CASE STUDY – Betty

Betty has a house worth $2,000,000, plus $300,000 of investments and $20,000 of personal assets. She currently receives a part pension of $1,048 per fortnight.

Betty would like to move into the luxury retirement village Ardency Kennedy Place. The apartment she is interested in has 3 bedrooms, 2 bathrooms, 2 car parks, and beautiful views across the landscaped courtyard.

Let's look at the different payment options available, noting that Kennedy Place offers three of the four Keyton Group payment options. The Pay As You Go option is not offered.

	Standard (DMF)	Prepaid plan	Refundable contribution
Ingoing			
Purchase price	$1,515,000	$1,802,850	$1,969,500
Establishment fee (non-refundable)	$0	$0	$68,932
Investments	$785,000	$497,150	$261,568
Personal assets	$20,000	$20,000	$20,000
Ongoing			
General service charge	$885 per month or $10,620 per year		
Pension	$0/year	$11,713/year	$28,514/year
Interest on investments at 4% p.a.	$31,400 /year	$19,886 /year	$10,463 /year
Betty's cash flow	**$20,780 /year**	**$21,135 /year**	**$28,357 /year**

	Standard (DMF)	Prepaid plan	Refundable contribution
Outgoing			
Sale price assuming 3% p.a. growth	$2,036,034		
DMF (30%)	$610,810	Paid upfront	$0
Reinstatement	$50,000	$50,000	$0
Long term maintenance fund (3%)	$61,081	$0	$0
Selling fees (assuming 2.5%)	$50,901	$50,901	$0
Exit amount in 10 years	**$1,263,242**	**$1,935,132**	**$1,969,500**
Guaranteed buyback/ refund	On settlement or as legislated	On settlement or as legislated	60 days

As you can see, the standard DMF option costs Betty the least upfront but the most when she leaves, giving her the most amount of money to invest or spend while she lives in the village but causing her to lose all of her pension entitlement. At the other end, the refundable contribution has the highest cost upfront, and gives her the most amount back, in the shortest period of time after she leaves. She also has certainty over the price she will pay as there is no sharing in capital gain or loss, and no reinstatement costs or selling fees — all of which could be different to the assumptions we have used for the estimates in the other two options. Under this option she receives the maximum age pension.

The prepaid plan enables Betty to pay her management fee, and in doing so save almost $323,000 compared with paying it when she leaves. This option also gives her almost $12,000 a year in pension (and access to the benefits that go with the concession card).

Ongoing costs

In a retirement village, regardless of the type of title held, residents are responsible for the ongoing costs of the village. These include insurance, water, rates, general lighting, staff wages, and repairs and maintenance. As these are reimbursable items, the village management is not allowed to make a profit on them, they can claim only the actual costs. The manager prepares a budget of expenditure for the year and each resident is levied for a proportion.

Methods used to determine each resident's proportion are similar to those used in body corporates. The most common approach is to base it on the size of your unit. This formula means that large units pay a higher levy than smaller units, which sometimes causes complaints from residents, if, for example, different-sized units have the same number of occupants but pay different shares of items such as water rates or staff salaries. Some villages set the fee per person. This is often the case where the general service charge incorporates meals or care, where it is clearly more expensive to have two residents rather than one.

In an LLC, the ongoing cost of living there is the site fee — the amount you pay to rent the land on which your house sits. Unlike a retirement village, the amount you pay is set by the operator and they are allowed to make a profit from site fees.

When budgeting for ongoing costs, you may wish to compare them with the costs of your own home, as well as the cost of any fitness and social club memberships that you won't need once you move to a village providing those facilities. In an LLC or strata title village the situation is also similar to the costs of living in your own home if you decide to leave: you, or your estate, are liable for these ongoing costs until resale of the home is finalised. In a retirement village in most states there are time limits on the period that you need to pay the general service charge after you leave the village. For example, in NSW the general service charge is only payable for a maximum of 42 days after you leave a retirement village.

In all types of retirement communities, residents are responsible for their personal living expenses such as medications and clothes. Expenses such as food, water and electricity may or may not be included in the regular fees.

Some of the newer communities are being built to be highly self-sufficient: harvesting rain water through tanks to care for gardens, wash laundry and flush toilets, and installing solar panels on the roofs to provide power to residents and the common areas of the village — it is even becoming common for villages to generate surplus power and sell their excess back to the grid.

Living Choice's **Fullarton Village** has what can only be described as a solar farm, with a whopping 785 solar panels across the roofs which are used to offset the community levies. In addition, the village has an agreement with Savant Energy to purchase power in bulk, which enables residents to get a cheaper price than if they were to negotiate individually. They have also used their collective bargaining power to get a cheaper deal on their internet through Uniti Wireless.

GemLife Moreton Bay sits on 149 hectares of bushland bursting with native birdlife, koalas and wetlands. Once built the community will have 553 homes — each with no rear neighbours — with more than 100 homes expected to have lake frontage on one of several lakes within the resort-style community.

Sustainability is at the heart of the community, with a significant proportion of all energy coming from on-site renewable generation and storage tanks to a market-leading solar energy and battery system. This will provide future residents with reduced energy bills.

The homes are planned to be electric vehicle-enabled, and there will also be a pool of EV vehicles for homeowner use. The homes themselves have been designed to harmonise with the resort's unique environment, and will be 7-star energy rated.

Another way to keep ongoing prices low is for retirement communities to provide extra services to their residents on a user-pays basis, through employees or external contractors with whom they can negotiate a better price through a bulk deal. Typical services include providing meals, cleaning and laundry services, and sometimes care.

CASE STUDY – Lisa

Lisa is a single pensioner who is looking to downsize. She expects to keep $1,100,000 from the sale of her home, after meeting selling and moving costs of $50,000. She has $150,000 in investments and $25,000 in personal assets, including her car.

The house she plans to buy is at Ingenia's Natura, in beautiful Port Stephens — a two-and-a half hour drive north of Sydney. It has 3 bedrooms, 2 bathrooms and a double garage, perfect for when her favourite grandson comes to stay. The price of the house is $965,000 and the site fees are $225/week.

Natura is a land lease community that is currently under development. Once complete it will have 111 2- and 3-bed homes, with prices ranging from $675,000 through to $1,050,000. The homes are made from sustainable materials and feature open-plan living areas to maximise natural light and airflow while merging indoor and outdoor living.

The clubhouse is the hub of community social life, and includes a communal alfresco dining space as well as private rooms for formal events or celebrations, a veggie garden and fire pit, a cinema, a bowling green and a wellness centre that includes an infinity edge heated lap pool, yoga and pilates studio, gym, and sauna. There is also a salon and consulting rooms.

Weekly site fees of $219–$225 per week cover costs to operate and maintain the community and facilities, as well as lease the land and pay council rates.

As an independent living community, assisted care is not a regular inclusion in the service delivery. However, the community management team provides free support services for residents through what's called Ingenia Activate, which includes social and lifestyle programs designed to keep residents healthy, active and entertained.

Selling her home to buy a house in the community will mean that Lisa will have an extra $135,000 to invest. Let's look at the effects of downsizing to Ingenia Natura on Lisa's asset position and annual cash flow.

	Stay at home	Downsize
Ingoing		
Purchase price	$1,100,000	$965,000
Investments	$150,000	$285,000
Personal assets	$25,000	$25,000
Ongoing		
Pension entitlement	$28,514	$28,514
Rent assistance	$0	$4,805
Investment return at 4%	$6,000 (on $150,000)	$11,400 (on $285,000)
Less Site fees	$0	− $11,700
Less Living expenses	− $30,000	− $25,000
Lisa's cash flow	**$4,514**	**$8,019**
Outgoing		
Sale price in 10 years' time	$1,478,308	$1,296,879
Marketing & sales commission (3%)	$44,349	$38,906
Final assets	**$1,433,959**	**$1,257,973**

When Lisa leaves the community and sells her home, she will receive the proceeds of the sale of her home, less any renovations she chooses to undertake and sales commission. There are no guaranteed buybacks in LLCs and — just like in a strata title — Lisa will need to continue paying her site fees until her home is sold.

Outgoing costs

A number of different costs may apply to the sale of your home within a retirement community. Understanding which ones will apply to you and how they are calculated is critically important. Ideally, you should understand what they are likely to be in dollar terms and how this relates to the sale price, so you can estimate your exit entitlement (that is, what you will have in your hand after you leave).

From the operator's point of view, the good thing about exit fees is that they are payable every time the unit changes hands. However, on average, independent living units resell every nine years and serviced apartments about every four years, so it is clear that developers have to be patient.

Deferred Management Fee (DMF)

Let's start with the DMF, which is the fee that causes the most confusion and is typically the biggest part of the exit fee. Traditionally, DMFs have been associated with retirement villages, but they also apply in some LLCs.

There are a number of possible components that make up the exit fee: deferred management fee, capital gain or loss, and selling costs are the most common. The DMF may be based on the purchase price, which means you always know what the cost will be, or on the sale price, which means you need to predict the price in the future. A good definition of the DMF is: "A fee fthat includes the operator's remuneration for providing community facilities, return for the financial risk taken to establish the village, and delayed payment for part of the purchase price until resale." Yes, that's a fancy way of saying "profit". But remember, retirement village operators may not make a profit on the initial sale and are not allowed to make a profit on the ongoing service fees, so the exit fee may represent their first, legitimate profit, not a final rip-off before you can escape their clutches.

To work out whether or not the DMF represents fair value, you need to look at the amount you have paid below the market price and the value of that money over time. For example, if the unit you are buying has a market price of $600,000 but you are only paying $500,000, then $100,000, plus the value of that money over the time you live in the village, will need to be recouped through the exit fee. If the operator expects residents to stay an average of 10 years, and has a value of capital of 8%, they will need to charge an exit fee of $200,000. They then need to add the profit that they weren't allowed to make on the service fees: $5,000/year would add $50,000 to the exit fee, giving a total of $250,000.

Capital gain (or loss)

The calculation of your exit fee may include a provision for sharing in any capital gain (or capital loss) with the operator. The share is not always the same: for example, your contract may provide for you to receive 50% of any capital gain but 100% of any capital loss. While many people think that property always goes up, they may have that impression because they haven't bought and sold many properties and those they have have been held for a long time. You also need to think about the fact that the value of retirement village units don't necessary move at the same rate or at the same time as the broader market. The

2022 PwC/Property Council Retirement Census released recently reveals the average cost of a two-bedroom Independent Living Unit in a retirement village grew by 6% over the 18 months to December 2022 to $516,000, while national house prices over the same period rose significantly by 26% to $831,900.

While it is not common, there are some contracts in which any share of capital gain or loss is calculated after the exit fee has been deducted. You are very unlikely to get any capital gain in this scenario, and in fact without significant capital growth you could easily be looking at a capital loss, even if the property value has actually increased in value!

Doing the calculations, or having a financial adviser do them for you, before you enter the contract means there will be no nasty surprises at the end.

Some people can get very caught up in wanting a contract that gives them some or all of the capital gain; as we have said before you need to balance that right out against your responsibilities and costs. As a general rule, you will find that contracts that give you some or all of the capital gain will also give you some or all of the costs associated with achieving that gain, and they often have a longer guaranteed buyback time frame, or no buyback at all. It's a good idea to do your sums based on a realistic long term capital gain assumption of, say, 2–3% per year, and then do the sums again for a gain of zero or even a loss, so you can see how the numbers look under different market conditions.

Selling costs

As part of selling the home — as with most real estate transactions — there can be refurbishment or reinstatement costs, and marketing expenses or sales commissions that the outgoing resident needs to pay.

Refurbishment costs vary enormously depending on what is needed. Obviously, a coat of paint and a few minor repairs is not going to be a huge cost, but renovating kitchens and bathrooms can cost tens of thousands. The retirement community operator would normally coordinate the trades required, but it is prudent to ask for a detailed quote of the works that will be undertaken, and the cost, before any work starts. If you don't agree on the scope or cost, discuss it with the operator. Be aware that you are not compelled to have the works carried out by their choice of trades if you don't wish.

Marketing expenses and sales commissions can also apply to the sale. The retirement community operator is normally best placed to manage and effect the sale. You can appoint your own agent — but we don't recommend it. First, most people who are considering moving to a retirement community make enquiries direct to the community, not with a real estate agent. Second, the sale contract for a retirement village or LLC is very different to other property contracts; it may be difficult for a real estate agent to understand and explain to prospective buyers. Third, retirement community units tend to be cheaper than most houses on the market, and real estate agents normally work on a sales commission, so they may prioritise other properties over yours. You are unlikely to save money by choosing a different sales agent. However, looking into it may put you in a better position to negotiate the marketing expenses and sales commission with the operator.

In some circumstances a departing resident and the retirement community operator cannot agree on the sale price that the home should be offered at; in such situations it may be necessary to engage a valuer, splitting that cost between the resident and the operator.

If your home doesn't sell

If your home is in an LLC and you can't sell it, or don't want to, you normally have greater flexibility in terms of what you can do. In many cases you will be able to keep the home and rent it out to an eligible resident. Obviously, this creates a situation where the property essentially has two landlords: you, the owner of the building, and the community operator, the owner of the land.

If you can't sell the home for the price you want, or you want to keep the home but no longer as part of the community, then you may want to look at moving it. This is not an exercise for the faint-hearted! While all of the homes are technically demountable, it is neither simple nor cheap to relocate them. You also need to think about whether the home will be more or less valuable to a buyer if it is in the community. As a general rule, the home will have a greater value being part of a community than as a stand-alone building. Unlike retirement villages, LLCs don't provide guaranteed buybacks.

Buybacks make retirement villages unlike most property transactions. They essentially mean that after you leave the village the operator can be required to buy your home if it hasn't sold within a certain amount of time. It's a bit like insurance: if your home sells then you have no need for the buyback because you get your money when it settles; it's only if your home doesn't sell that the village operator buys it back from you.

The conditions under which you are entitled to a buyback and the time limit are specified by state-based legislation. Broadly speaking, the timeframe ranges from 18 months in South Australia and Queensland to no mandatory buyback (except if you're moving into aged care) in Victoria. In New South Wales there is a 6-month buyback in metropolitan areas and 12 months in regional areas.

While legislation sets the conditions and time limits for buybacks, as you will see in the examples, you can find villages that will give you a shorter buyback period or offer a buyback when the legislation does not require it. The timeframe may also depend on the contract you choose. At time of writing, the shortest buyback on offer, where no buyback is required, is 3 months.

What is a buyback worth?

A big part of the value of a buyback is the "pillow factor", knowing that if your home in the village doesn't sell within a certain amount of time you (or your estate) will get your exit entitlement regardless.

If your next move is to aged care, then the value of your buyback can be significant in dollar terms. Most people who move into aged care pay the market price for their accommodation, which typically starts around $500,000 in metropolitan areas, but can go as high as $3 million if you have views of Sydney Harbour. As we explain in *Chapter 16*, any amount of the lump sum refundable accommodation deposit (RAD) that you don't pay attracts interest at a government set rate, currently 8.15% per year, so it pays to look at your buyback in those terms. Just say your exit entitlement from a retirement village was going to be $400,000 with an 18-month buyback, each day of that wait would represent a daily accommodation payment to the aged care facility of $89 per day. So the full 18 months would cost you $48,900.

This can be an important consideration when comparing retirement village costs.

CASE STUDY — Sophia

Sophia is looking at moving to a retirement village. She has identified two villages that she likes; each one has a unit with a purchase price of $500,000 and an exit fee of 30% after 10 years (3% per year for a maximum of 10 years). With modest capital growth, Sophia estimates each unit would sell for $600,000 in ten years' time.

There are a few little differences in the contracts. In the first village, the exit fee is based on the purchase price; in the second it is based on the sale price. In village 1 the operator takes all of the capital gain and meets all of the selling costs (renovation costs, marketing fees and sales costs). In village 2 they share the capital gain with the resident 50:50, but the resident meets the costs of selling. While Sophia doesn't need to renovate her unit in village 1 she does need to do some minor works (painting and steam cleaning) after she leaves. With village 1 Sophia knows what her exit entitlement will be before she moves in and has a six-month guaranteed buyback if her unit doesn't sell. With village 2 there are a number of variables that could affect her exit entitlement including the capital gain or loss on her unit, the cost of renovations, and marketing and selling fees. Also, the buyback period for her unit is 18 months, 12 months longer than village 1.

It goes to show that two units that may look the same on the surface (having the same purchase price and 30% DMF) can have very different rights, responsibilities and costs.

	Village 1	Village 2
Purchase price	$500,000	$500,000
Sale price in 10 years' time	$600,000	$600,000
Deferred management fee 30%	$150,000 Based on purchase price	$180,000 Based on resale price
Capital gain share	$0	$50,000 (50%)
Renovation/ refurbishment	$2,000 Reinstate	$50,000 Renovate
Sales commission at 2%	$0	$12,000
Marketing fees	$0	$4,000
Exit entitlement	$348,000	$354,000
Guaranteed buyback	6 months	18 months

Here's how the numbers are calculated.

Village 1

First calculate the exit fee. Based on the purchase price, the DMF is 30% of $500,000, which is $150,000.

Subtract the exit fee from the purchase price, which gives $350,000. Sophia's share of capital gain is zero, likewise her selling costs are limited to a reinstatement cost of $2,000. Sophia's exit entitlement would be $348,000.

Village 2

Again, start by calculating the exit fee. Based on the sale price, the DMF is 30% of $600,000, which is $180,000.

Then calculate Sophia's share of capital gain: $600,000 sale price minus $500,000 purchase price gives a capital gain of $100,000; half of which is Sophia's share.

So the total exit fee is the DMF of $180,000, plus the operator's share of capital gain, $50,000, giving $230,000. Subtract the exit fee from the sale price and you have $370,000. When you also deduct the renovation cost, sales commission and marketing fees, Sophia's exit entitlement would be $354,000.

While the numbers we have used create an outcome under each that is quite similar in dollar terms, the difference between the two contracts could easily add up over 10 years to a difference more like $50,000, depending on the amount of any capital gain or loss and the selling costs.

In addition, if she has to wait the maximum of 6 or 18 months for her exit entitement, at current rates, village 2's contract will cost her an extra $29,100.

Affordable housing

Some retirement villages and LLCs are specifically intended to provide affordable housing to their residents. Others designate a number of homes within the community to provide housing at a reduced price, with the others being offered at market price.

So, what is "affordable housing"? Sometimes it involves the village operator undertaking an assessment of your financial position to determine that you meet their criteria, often using a copy of your Centrelink assessment to verify your assets and income. The village operator will then offer you a unit either to rent or to buy on the basis of what you can afford to pay.

Essentially, retirement communities charge an exit fee so that their offer is more affordable to prospective residents. In this way, the standard model is basically affordable housing: they are letting you pay less upfront and more at the end. Whether or not it is *actually* affordable depends on your personal circumstances. Growth in housing prices and changes to how the pension is calculated mean that, for a significant number of prospective residents, this model isn't really affordable at all. Of course, the amount the operator collects at the end needs to account for the amount you didn't pay upfront and what they could have earned on that money over that time; depending on the value they put on that capital it may be more affordable for you to pay the true price upfront.

When it comes to LLC's, the fact that you are buying the home and renting the land on which it sits can make it significantly cheaper than buying a house and land. Add to this the fact that many LLC residents are able to claim rent assistance to assist in meeting the weekly or monthly site fees and you have an option that can be far more affordable.

It's important to understand that an affordable housing offer may not mean that you will pay a very small amount, it may simply mean that you pay less than the market price on entry, and a higher exit fee later. In the not-for-profit sector, the affordable housing options tend to work on either a 50% DMF or a donation basis, which is another way of saying that the exit fee is 100%.

For example, the retirement village may offer units at a market price of $440,000 with an exit fee of 30% after 10 years, based on the purchase price, but this resident can only pay $350,000. The village operator will consider how long the resident is likely to live in the village, work out the value of capital over that period, then adjust the resident's exit fee to compensate themselves for this lost value.

Let's assume the operator's value of capital is 7%, that is, if the resident paid $440,000 and lived in the community for 10 years, the operator would earn 7% income each year on the entry free, and an exit fee of $132,000 after 10 years. If the resident pays only $350,000 for the same unit on entry, they would need to pay an exit fee of $219,044 after 10 years to compensate the operator. Why is it so high? Simply because of the time value of money. The operator is making the same amount of money.

TABLE 10: *Cost comparison — exit fees giving the same operator return for different entry fees*

	Market price	Alternative payment plan
Entry fee	$440,000	$350,000
Exit fee after 1 year	$12,300	$19,500
Exit fee after 5 years	$66,000	$102,320
Exit fee after 10 years	$132,000	$219,044

Now let's look at it more closely from the operator's point of view. If the resident leaves the village inside the 10 years then offering this alternative payment plan means that they are no better or worse off than if the resident paid the market price. But if the resident lives in the village for more than 11 years they will start to lose money compared with the market price arrangement. While it is unlikely the operator would ever discuss it, when considering such an arrangement the operator will normally take into account how long they expect the resident to remain in the village.

Rental, plus entry and exit fees

In some retirement villages your purchase price is based on your assets, but deliberately kept below the homeowner's entry contribution limit of $242,000; then you pay ongoing rent. The purchase price is deliberately kept at or below the threshold so that you can qualify as a non-homeowner for pension purposes and be eligible for rent assistance.

In most cases the amount you pay will be completely exhausted during the period of your stay. For many people the idea of paying an exit fee of 100% can be a shock, especially when other units within the same village have an exit fee of 25% or 30%, but don't get hung up on the percentages: work it out in dollar terms. 100% of $100,000 is cheaper than 30% of $450,000. Bear in mind that if you are considering entering an agreement to pay an exit fee of 100%, you probably don't have the means to pay the market price on entry.

For example, you may have assets of $150,000 and agree with the village operator to pay $100,000 as your purchase price. Normally the village operator may sell the same unit for $400,000 with a 30% exit fee. Instead, they will sell the unit to you for $100,000 with a 100% exit fee. As discussed above, while on the surface it may seem that the operator is only forgoing $20,000, they are actually losing much more than this due to the time value of money, i.e. the income they can earn on the $300,000 for the period that you are living in the village. For this reason, many village operators will also charge a rent on the unit. Knowing that the resident has limited financial means and will most likely be eligible for rent assistance, rent is often set at a percentage of the full pension plus rent assistance. For example, 50% of the pension plus rent assistance would mean that a single person's rent is $306/week. While this doesn't fully compensate the operator for not having access to an extra $300,000 of capital, it does go some way to bridging the gap. For many operators, providing affordable housing is less about generating the same return as a market price, and more about meeting a need within the community or honouring a moral or religious code of conduct.

Pure rental

In some cases, either because the operator has decided to charge on a rental basis or because the resident cannot afford to pay a lump sum towards the cost of their accommodation, housing is provided purely on a rental basis. Some villages also include packages of meals and care in the rent.

Ingenia Communities have 25 **Ingenia Gardens** rental communities across Australia. People moving into these communities have the option of renting their unit and self-catering, or purchasing a lunch package which provides a two-course lunch 7 days a week. The Ingenia Gardens community at Dubbo has units for $387 per week for a single person and $436 per week for a couple; the price to have lunch included is $447 per week for a single and $556 per week for a couple. That's $60 for a full week's lunches!

Such a model works on economies of scale: pooling residents' funds enables food to be bought and prepared for less than the ingredients alone would cost each household buying small amounts on a retail basis. If you're a single pensioner this model means you could receive $1,097 per fortnight in pension plus rent assistance, and after you pay for your accommodation and meals you would have about $387 a fortnight for other expenses.

Eureka Villages specialises in rental villages for independent seniors. With over 40 villages nationally, they are Australia's largest owner, operator and developer of rental retirement communities. The majority of Eureka Villages have 50–60 purpose-built, low maintenance units, set among gardens with a centrally located hub that houses the community room, dining area, lounge, laundry and village manager's office. All of the villages are pet friendly, and most offer chef-prepared meals on-site for residents and their loved ones.

Residents rent under a Residential Tenancy Agreement, with security of tenure for as long as residents wish to renew their leases. Average weekly rents ranging from $300–$460 per week include meals, village maintenance, and management of the community as a whole.

Department of Housing involvement

In some cases, affordable housing is co-ordinated entirely by the village operator; in others, the Department of Housing maintains a waiting list on behalf of the village. This is typically a service for people who are homeless, or at risk of homelessness.

You will normally need to complete paperwork showing your age and that of the people who live with you, what your financial means are, any pets, any health conditions they need to be aware of and the location of your preferred housing. When suitable accommodation becomes available within the village, the Department of Housing, the village operator, or both will contact you.

The amount you pay will normally depend on your financial means. The operator will often set a rental amount they believe is affordable as a percentage of your income — anything between 30% (for accommodation only) and 85% (where meals and other services are included) is common. Again, make sure you know what income is included in the assessment of your financial means.

The affordable housing model that operates in up to 50 units in IRT Group retirement villages works on 30% of the resident's total income, based on the income recorded by Centrelink.

CASE STUDY — Beth

Beth, aged 79, has $25,000 in the bank and $2,000 in personal effects. This is how her income would be assessed by Centrelink, as a single person. IRT uses a similar formula. Her $25,000 would be deemed to earn 0.25%. So her deemed income would be $62.50/year. She would receive the full pension of $1,064/fortnight, which is $27,664/year. Based on this, Beth qualifies for an affordable housing unit with IRT, where rent is set at 30% of resident income. So her rent would be calculated as $27,726.50 x 30% = $8,318/year, or $160/week.

On the basis that the rent is $160/week, she would also be entitled to rent assistance of $132/fortnight, or $3,444/year, but this is not included in the calculation of income.

Obviously, such a rent is almost impossible to find elsewhere, so it goes without saying that IRT's affordable housing program is designed to help those who truly need it — and that all of the units are currently occupied. There is always a waitlist, and priority on it is based on level of need.

11

RETIREMENT COMMUNITY CONTRACTS

Now you understand about the different types of retirement communities and have an overview of your care options and costs, let's look at the various forms of contracts used by retirement communities and what these mean for you. Your contract sets out your rights, responsibilities and costs, so it is critical that you understand it. Remember too, that the laws vary from state to state. Try not to get hung up on any one item, such as avoiding an exit fee or sharing in capital gain, but keep your eye on the big picture to ensure that your needs are met overall.

Retirement villages

There are currently five types of retirement village contract: leasehold, licence, company or unit trust title, strata title, and rental. Some villages offer a variety of arrangements in a single community.

Let's look at each type of contract in more detail.

Leasehold

This is the most common form of contract, particularly for privately owned and publicly listed retirement villages. When you move into the village you pay an agreed sum in exchange for a 99-year lease. This lease naturally lasts for your lifetime and, if a couple take out the lease and one dies, it continues to the death of the other partner. Your lease is registered on the title deed, but when you die the rights die with you. Your exit entitlement is normally paid to you, or to your estate, either when your unit is sold to the next resident or at the end of a guaranteed buyback period, if the unit has not sold. The amount you will receive depends on your agreement with the operator.

Licence

When the right to occupy the unit is granted by a licence instead of a lease, you lend the developer an agreed sum, and in return you are allowed to live in the property. This is commonly used by churches, charities or not-for-profit organisations who are operating a retirement village. You are entitled to live in the unit for life, but you are not registered on the title deed. However, your rights under the licence are recognised by law, so effectively you are in the same position as if you had a registered lease. Just like a lease arrangement, the amount you will receive after you exit, and when, depends on your agreement with the operator.

Company/unit trust title

Contracts that operate on company title or unit trust title mean that you buy shares in a company or units in a trust for the right to occupy your unit and use the communal facilities. When you leave the village, your shares are sold either to the incoming resident or back to the company.

Strata title

With a strata title you have title to your home. It is not quite the same as owning your own home, because the operator usually specifies that you have to sell it to someone who meets the guidelines for residency. Also, you may not be able to borrow against the property, as the operator may take a charge over the title to ensure you pay the exit fee when you leave. And if you decide to bequeath the property to a child (or someone else) who meets the criteria to live in the village, the exit fee will still apply to the transfer of the property.

Body corporate committees typically end up being controlled by a handful of people, and squabbles and difficulties arise as people, typically with no expertise in running such a committee, try to work together. Historically, strata villages have run into all these problems. Legislative changes and changes to the tax treatment of leasehold and licence arrangements for operators has now seen most strata villages convert to leasehold or licence arrangements.

Running a village that contains many units, as well as community facilities such as tennis courts and swimming pools, requires money and skill. If expensive works are required on any of the community infrastructure, you will need to contribute to a special levy (a one-off amount in addition to your normal fees) to fund the work.

To ease the likelihood of issues arising, and ensure that the village is managed professionally, many of the operators that own and operate strata villages now run the owners corporation and provide that service to the residents for free or at a substantial discount to what it would cost to use an alternate provider. If a village gains a reputation for being poorly managed, or having a troublesome body corporate, particularly if residents do not have any guaranteed buyback, they can be stuck with a unit that is worth less than they paid for it, and which may be hard to sell. In most states, strata title villages are not subject to guaranteed buyback provisions, so if you are thinking about moving into a strata village make sure you know whether you will be getting a guaranteed buyback or not.

Jan @ Bolton Clarke, Europa

Moving here has been a new lease on life.

I had always loved where I lived, but my last house? I just didn't love it, and I loved the maintenance even less. Having said that, I wasn't looking to downsize to a retirement village!

My daughter lived in an apartment next door to the village when it was being built. She was worried how high it was going to be and whether it was going to affect her views. Then one day we went out for lunch and she said, "Maybe we should go in and have a look." We spoke to the manager and salesperson, and they showed us the facilities and about six different apartments. As soon as I saw my apartment I thought, "It's this or nothing".

I think starting the process was the hardest part: I didn't sleep too well. I was worried about the money; I didn't want to be here and be poor. I'm a single person. I get an age pension and top it up from my super, so I needed to be sure that I could afford it. Chris, the salesperson, gave me a copy of *Downsizing Made Simple* to help me understand how it all works. The book was such a help, it was a step-by-step guide that was easy to follow — how to declutter, how the contracts work, how to think about the money side of things, what it costs, how it affects your pension … the whole process. It's such a daunting thing.

Bolton Clarke gave me two different payment options. I took the one that has the lowest exit fee, it doesn't have capital gain or loss and I get a guaranteed buyback after six months. I liked the certainty of that and the fact that my monthly service fee is set for life. I thought about it for a while, and spoke to a family friend who told me to call Rachel. She let me know that I could get a Village Guru report that would crunch the numbers on the village costs and my pension for me, which I did. When I saw that she was booked in to give a talk at the village I made sure to get along to it.

Chris invited me to the happy hours, before I had even signed anything, so I came along and asked the people already living here whether they liked it: they all loved it. Having a light and bright apartment was important to me — my apartment faces north. It looks over the street and gets the morning sun, but in the afternoon it's shaded from westerly sun.

I thought, I need to discuss this with my three kids. So we sat down and I went through the financial arrangements with them. They were wonderful, they said, "Whatever you want to do is up to you. We want you to be happy: it's your money." So I put a refundable deposit down of $2,000. Once my house sold I needed to pay another $8,000, and then the rest on settlement. My contract for my apartment was conditional on selling my house. I thought, if I can't sell my house to pay for this and all the other fees — lawyers, agent fees, new furniture — then I won't do it. It all adds up — I suppose it's cost about $50,000.

I didn't want an auction, I didn't want to pay for photos and marketing and all of that, and I didn't want hoards of people traipsing through my home every weekend. I spoke to a local agent who was great. He said, let's just list it for private sale and see what sort of interest we get, and it sold in 10 days to a single lady with a dog, who bought it for all the same reasons I did.

I got a good price, and that means that I'm comfortable — I've got a good buffer. I've kept my pension, and I've got some extra money in the bank so I can afford to go on a holiday or whatever I want to do.

I got rid of all my furniture and got all new stuff. I had a lot of antiques with a lot of memories, so it was hard to part with it. My niece bought a big farmhouse in the country and had no furniture, so she has most of my furniture there, where it looks lovely and I can visit it.

I hadn't bought furniture for 45 years, so I went to an interior decorator to get some help and ideas about what would look nice and what would fit well in the space. I have everything new, modern and lovely. The crowning glory was that Europa offered a $10,000 voucher for Handled with Care removalists: they packed up everything and then brought it here and unpacked it all for me. They also arranged hard rubbish pickups and took things to auction rooms and op shops … it just made it so much easier — the older you get the harder it is.

Finding my village was a coincidence, it was just because my daughter lived next door. I didn't look at anything else, I knew this was perfect. People said, "You should look at others," but I knew it was the right one for me.

Moving here has been a new lease on life, like a new chapter starting. I hadn't had a new house since I was in my 30s, everything is beautiful, modern and new — it gives you a lift. And it's nice being part of a community. We have morning teas, and I am in the garden club (we have vegetable gardens on the roof-top and we share the produce among the residents) and we have happy hours each week. Being here I'm closer to my sister and close to public transport — I jump on the tram, which is two steps from the front door and head into town to visit the galleries, go to a show or to the football, which is a whole family affair, we go most weeks and we have lunch or dinner together.

While I'm in the hustle and bustle of St Kilda, I feel safe and I know that my car is safe in the carpark underneath. There's a lovely park up the road that I take my dog Dorothy to almost every day and we walk around the area. She's been my companion for 12 years, I wouldn't have moved here without her. And of course, my daughter lives just next door so I see her nearly every day.

Jan and her dog Dorothy

I think the key is that you don't want to leave it too long, it's hard enough, but if you didn't have the physical or mental strength it would be very hard. You have to make an effort; you have to be proactive and take the help that's there, reading books like *Downsizing Made Simple*, and thinking about what you want the future to look like.

I helped my mum move from the family home into aged care in her 90s. She didn't want to go, and it was hard. I didn't want to be like that. I'm a fit and healthy 78, and don't need any care. I didn't want to live anywhere that I didn't feel at home. But I didn't want to be isolated in my home. There's not many places like this. I have a luxury apartment, but I know if I need it I can get care — some people here already do. I don't intend to move again. I still like my own space, I'm used to my own company and I enjoy it every day. My kids are happy I've made the move too. They come over, and the grandkids come over and we have meals, they are happy for me. I think there is a bit of relief for them, knowing that I'm safe and I'm happy.

I think moving to a village is not a financial decision, it's a lifestyle decision. Whatever's left when I leave here is a bonus for the kids. I would be horrified if they thought differently.

Rental

While traditionally churches and the charitable sector have been the main providers of rental retirement accommodation, there are a few private sector rental villages around.

Rental villages tend to operate under one of two models: a subsidised rental model for people with few assets whose income is fixed, often including entitlement to government rent assistance; and a market price model for people who choose to rent their unit, paying a higher ongoing cost but with far less paid upfront and no exit fee.

If you are looking for a retirement village unit to rent, you should be aware that villages consisting solely of rentals tend to be small. Rent is usually relatively high, because you are effectively paying the rent for your unit, plus the service charges for the community, and compensation to the operator for not receiving any lump sum or exit fees. And, just like a normal rental, you are responsible for all your personal outgoings such as food, water, electricity, insurance and telephone. In addition, if the village provides you with meals or personal services, these are usually an additional cost.

While rental retirement villages often look just like any other retirement village, with communal areas and social activities, you need to make sure you understand whether you are a tenant or a resident, as they are legally different. As a resident, you are covered by the *Retirement Villages Act* and the consumer protection rules within it. As a tenant you sign a residential tenancy agreement, on a fixed or periodic basis, and are covered by the state-based residential tenancies act and authority. This legislation is the same as if you rented a private home, and your tenancy agreement can be ended at any time, depending on the terms specified in the agreement. A tenancy agreement may also require you to lodge a security deposit with the Residential Tenancies Bond Authority, normally equal to four weeks' rent.

Some large villages, in which most units are under leasehold or licence arrangements, set aside a few places for rent by people who cannot afford the standard arrangement. Often these arrangements work on a combination of an upfront payment, sometimes with a much higher exit fee (in some cases 100% of the upfront payment), and an ongoing rent. The entry fee is normally based on the resident's ability to pay, while the rent is often a percentage of the full pension plus the maximum rental assistance, regardless of the actual amount the resident is entitled to receive.

In contrast to all of the licence, loan and lease arrangements, a rental model may seem easier and cheaper. But considering the long run is the key with a rental village. As we have pointed out, renting in a retirement village can be the same as renting anywhere else and if your tenancy agreement is short — say, 12 months — where will you move to if it is not renewed?

Retirement Village Code of Conduct

In 2020 the Property Council introduced a Retirement Village Code of Conduct. The code locks villages into a range of commitments and processes to keep villages focusing on the wellbeing of residents, prioritising transparency and fairness, and resolving disputes well.

The aim of the code is to ensure that villages:

- promote and protect the interests of residents (current and future)
- provide clarity and transparency, particularly with sales contracts and obligations
- implement consistently high standards across the whole transaction (moving into, living in, and leaving).

A code administrator is responsible for ensuring that villages signed up to the code complete annual compliance checks, maintain a code complaints and breach register, and report publicly on the volume and nature of complaints.

Mike @ Anglicare, The Ponds

We knew it was important to make the transition.

We had been living in our house for 20 years, having downsized from the family home when our four daughters moved out. But it still had 4 bedrooms, 3 bathrooms and included in-law accommodation. It was becoming a chore to clean, and the lawns and garden needed constant work. The sloping driveway was a hazard that claimed one broken ankle, and despite the new side stairs was a challenge for us to get up and down safely.

The fences needed replacing, the roof had leaked during recent heavy rain and the hot water system had to be replaced. I wasn't getting up ladders even to change a lightbulb or smoke detector any more!

We knew that all of these issues would be solved if we moved to a village and the fortnightly fee would simply replace what we had been spending one way or another anyway.

We worked together for almost 30 years in two businesses and decided to sell the last one in 2016, which was a catalyst for thinking about what our next step was. We knew we had to downsize again at some stage. Sandra had spinal surgery, which was successful, but after two weeks at home she had a fall and fractured her femur ... that accelerated our plans.

One option was to downsize in the same area, but there was nothing suitable on one level, which was now critical. Very few conventional homes are age friendly, and such a move would only be delaying the inevitable.

We looked at three independent living villages. One was a vertical village, close by with many people we knew in there. We could have signed up then and there for the third stage and we would be in there now. But Sandra did not like the vertical style, she wanted space for her plants and a clothesline (we only use a drier when necessary, it's the original thinking of wind and solar).

The second place was an older village, full of people much older than us. It did not have the same vibe as the first, but would have been OK financially. Our eldest daughter ruled it out as it was too far from her place.

We looked at the third and final village, which was Stage 6 of The Ponds, an Anglicare village with a co-located care facility. Stage 6 was 50 new duplex villas, the last stage of 250 homes.

We had a coffee with the representative in the morning and signed up that afternoon. The vibe was right, and we had our 2.5-bedroom villa locked in, close to the amenities block.

The entry price was flexible in that they offered three DMF options, and we could make that final choice a very short time before we were to move in. We had an idea of what we could get for our house, but liked the flexibility of the choices that Anglicare provided.

We had an approximate timeline for the move so we started de-cluttering (you can never start that too early)! We had to make the house sale-ready, and the local charities appreciated our extras. We decided to lose most of our furniture and buy new for our new smaller home. Most of our big appliances — the fridge and washing machine — would have needed replacing soon anyway. This also made the moving plan easier. Still, we had lots of boxes in the garage, ready to move. An almost-empty house was easy to get painted, and that was money well spent!

Mike and his wife Sandra

We had no idea how much our house would sell for, so we sought advice from the local real estate guru for our suburb, who surprised us with his estimate. As it turns out, we exceeded his upper figure on the day. I would advise anyone to do this exercise sooner rather than later, so you have some planning guide for the auction.

We took his advice to get the place styled, again, that was money well spent. With a timeline in place, we decided to put the house on the market with a longer settlement period. House prices were going up, interest rates were rising, and a recession was on the horizon. The open houses were a challenge with having to pack up the cat in a cage, remove all personal belongings and drive around the block, all for a 20-minute open house!

Over a few weeks we had 100 groups through, and on auction day there were seven registered bidders. There was some last minute drama — two of the keen bidders wanted an earlier settlement: three months instead of six. Knowing that would be critical to the best price, we agreed, and it paid off — we sold at $1.45 M, some of the earlier offers were as low as $900K.

The early settlement changed our plans drastically, as the new place would not be ready. Covid and the war in Ukraine had disrupted the supply chain, creating construction delays. We had factored in an interim plan for storage and temporary accommodation: somewhere furnished if it was a longer time or a budget hotel if it was short term.

We still stayed in a hotel for two nights ahead of the settlement. This reduced the stress of moving, leaving time for moving almost everything to storage and getting professional cleaners in. Same-day settlements can be very stressful, so we wanted to take as much of the pressure out of it as possible.

Then the bombshell came!

Anglicare let us know that their builder had gone broke and there was going to be a nine-month delay for our villa. We suddenly faced a stressful search for a 2-bedroom rental with a cat, and half our furniture in storage. The good news was that the higher interest rates on the money we got for the house more than covered the extra costs of rental and storage.

Despite the delay, we knew it was important to make the transition. We had already moved in mentally and we were going to everything we could at the village. We got to know many people ahead of time, especially our cohort of fellow Stage 6 residents. I am very involved in the local community and away from home quite a bit with meetings and conferences, so Sandra needs other people's company.

The financial planning still had to be done. Anglicare uses the Village Guru software so you can see clearly what the numbers look like across their different options. You put in the sale price, or expected price, then add your personal numbers, and it gives you some great information about what it's going to cost to live in the village and how it can affect your pension. Once we understood that we sought financial planning advice, which is worth the investment. There are advisers who specialise in this stage of your life, and it's worth talking to them. Getting this wrong can cost you a lot of money.

Land lease communities

When it comes to your legal contract to live in an LLC, it will depend on whether you are a renter or a land lease community homeowner.

Most people are homeowners, but it is important to understand that there are two separate components: the contract for your home and the contract to lease (rent) your land.

The contract for your home is likely to be a single transaction if you are buying a home that is already built, but if you are building your home the contract is likely to be a little more complex — involving a number of transactions including the initial deposit, progress payments and a final payment upon completion.

The contract for your land will be typically be a long term lease arrangement, however, you can agree to minimum term of at least three years. The leasehold arrangements tend to be not much different to those in a retirement village, except that the contract is over the land rather than the dwelling, and in some cases the leasehold periods are shorter — somewhere between 50 and 99 years is standard, although some leases are shorter with a guaranteed renewal. The terms of the leasehold will include a full list of conditions about living in the community, your right to sell your home when you want to leave and how increases to the site fees apply. For example, they may be indexed each year in line with the consumer price index (CPI) or a fixed rate like 3% per year, or they may be changed by notice and linked to a "market price", which means that the price paid by the last person to enter the village will determine the price you pay when your site fees are indexed.

If the lease for your land is offered on a short term lease (three years), then it represents many of the same pros and cons as it does in a retirement village, but on a much bigger scale. If you own your home but rent your land and the lease is not renewed, where are you going to put your house? While, technically, homes in an LLC can be "demounted", doing so is a complex and expensive exercise. Save yourself a lot of headache, heartache and money by having a lease that fits with how long you intend to remain living there.

Of course, there are homes for rent in LLCs too. The key difference between a rental home in an LLC and one in the suburbs is that in addition to the rental agreement you will also need to abide by the community rules. Under a rental agreement you don't purchase the home or pay sites fees, you rent both the home and the land from the operator.

Di @ Ingenia Lifestyle, Lara

My downsizing story is a bit of a funny one.

My husband semi-retired a few years ago … for some reason we just couldn't get along and we both thought the other had changed. In the end we decided to separate. It's something I never would have predicted and certainly came as a big shock to our family and friends. We didn't want to fight and waste money on lawyers so we agreed on a property settlement — that way we knew what we could each afford, and we could get on with our lives.

It was hard to live under the same roof, so I wondered: where do I go? what do I do? What I knew for sure was that I wanted to stay in the area, and I wanted somewhere I felt safe.

I had driven past the village a lot of times but this one day I decided to go in and have a look. It ticked a lot of boxes — it was where I wanted to be (location), it was a safe secure community (the gates are locked every night, and everyone looks out for each other) and the house was affordable.

It was perfect, so I didn't look at anywhere else; normally I probably would have shopped around but … this was perfect. There were no houses built, just the designs — and the prices were great. I put a deposit on straight away. It was important to me that I moved to a lifestyle village: it's not an old people's home or a "retirement village" … that's not me — I might not work but I'm not old!

We were each separately planning our next move. But I went home that day and I asked, "Where do you think you will go?" and he said that he was thinking Lara Lifestyle Village. I said, "I just bought a house there today,"

In December 2016 I moved into the village. He kept living in our old home and then moved in with his daughter until May 2017, when he moved into the village ... four houses away! I remember thinking, "Oh God, now he is my neighbour!"

It wasn't too bad. We caught up occasionally for lunch and the conversation would often turn to "where did it all go wrong" for us. We didn't have any answers.

In the meantime, my dad got sick and then I got sick. During my illness my "ex" came over to check up on me — he cared for me. Going through that I could see that we still had something.

In Feb 2018 we got back together. Ironically, the catalyst was him finally reading a letter I gave him for our anniversary in December 2016 after we had separated. In it I spoke about how moving to the village might be the way back for us.

We agreed to take it slow.

The next month there was an open day at the village where they were showing the new homes. At the time he was in a 1-bed house and I was in a 2-bedder. When we went and had a look, we just loved the Maple, which has 2 bedrooms + study — so we bought it.

We each sold our homes — for $255,000 and $220,000 respectively — so we made about $50,000 on the sale of our homes. Of course, I am not saying that people should or would want to go through this as a money-making exercise, and it may be different for others, but we have been fortunate. When we bought our new home together, we had some money left over. Rent assistance has also been a huge benefit in terms of making it affordable: it makes a difference of between $100 and $200 per week.

Back together, Di and her husband outside their home at Ingenia Lifestyle Lara

The time apart did us both good. Had we not split we wouldn't have ended up in the village — so every cloud has a silver lining.

Living in the village allows us each to be more of an individual; we each get time (and the facilities are right under our noses) to enjoy the things we like to do separately as well as together. I have learnt that I can be independent, and I will be fine, but at the end of the day I have also learnt that having the right person by your side is the most important thing. He's never home: he's out with the boys playing pool, doing men's group things; and I am the secretary of the resident's committee, which keeps me busy and enables me to give back to the village.

We have never had so many friends. It's funny, when we travel, we miss our friends and being part of the village. Everyone moves for different reasons; this community couldn't have been better for me.

I think the best gauge of a village is to speak to the other residents. Get along to a BBQ — there's always plenty of things like that going on. Don't judge it from the outside. A lot of people think about it and talk about it, but they don't do any more than that — my advice would be, have a look!

2023 update

Like everyone else, we survived the Covid pandemic. The resident committee that was there folded and I'm no longer in it, but we have a new committee now with new ideas and new energy. Bruce is back playing pool most days and he visits a couple of our older neighbours.

We have navigated through a few health issues over the last few years. I had both my knees replaced in 2022 which has slowed me down a little, so I have been focused on getting back on my feet (pardon the pun) and enjoying life. We have been using Ingenia

Connect, which connects people with care. I am doing hydrotherapy through that and Bruce is registered to start with a gym session next week. We are on the list for some extra home help too, some grab rails for the bathroom and some help with cleaning the house. These were things we didn't want or need when we moved in, but it's been good to have them there and to know if we need more in the future they will help us to add on what we need.

At the moment we are focused on making up for lost time during Covid: we are heading up to Queensland in a couple of weeks. So that will be lovely: sitting on the balcony enjoying the sun (and maybe a glass of wine), and watching the surfers. Beyond that we have a cruise to look forward to in December, we are just catching up on holidays at the moment.

As for as our relationship, we are great. I mean — don't get me wrong — we have our moments like everyone does, but it's much better to be going through life with him than without him.

While you would never wish to separate, I don't regret it; it brought us here and I don't know if that would have happened otherwise. I think it all happens for a reason.

Summary of contract types

Which contract type is best? That is something you will have to decide for yourself; they all have pros and cons. Keep in mind that the factors that make living in a village enjoyable are not the financial ones. It's good management, good facilities and good neighbours that make life a pleasure.

Fundamentally, your contract is a balance of rights, responsibilities and costs. It is important not to get hung up on one aspect but to view it from all three angles. For example, many people get fixated on having a contract that gives them the right to some or all of the capital gain, but ignore the associated responsibilities to compensate the operator for any capital loss and meet the costs associated with renovating and selling the property.

The complaints we hear most commonly are about unresponsive managers, "unfair" rises in ongoing costs, and how long it takes to get their money when people leave a retirement community. So make sure you pay attention to these factors.

To help you get and keep your head around the various options, we have created tables that summarise the rights, responsibilities and costs of both retirement villages and LLCs. These are based on typical contracts under NSW law. Always check specifics for your state or territory and your preferred retirement communities.

TABLE 11: Summary of rights, responsibilities and costs in retirement villages, under the Retirement Villages Act 1999 (NSW)

	Lease (registered interest holder)	Lease/ licence (non-registered interest holder)	Company title scheme	Strata scheme	Rental
Age restriction	Yes	Yes	Yes	Yes	Yes
Right to occupy	Permanent	Permanent	Permanent	Permanent	Temporary
Maximum or typical term of contract	99 years or for life	99 years or for life	Until property is sold	Until property is sold	As per contract
Ownership of property/title registration	Operator	Operator	Operator	Resident	Operator
Ingoing					
Stamp duty	No	No	No	Yes	No
Deposit	Yes	Yes	Yes	Yes	Bond
Deposit refund	Yes	Yes	As per contract	As per contract	Yes
Minimum time to consider documents	14 days	14 days	14 days	14 days	14 days
Contracts to sign	Lease	Lease or contract to occupy	Contract to buy shares Contract for services	Contract to buy property Contract for services	Lease or licence to occupy

	Lease (registered interest holder)	Lease/ licence (non-registered interest holder)	Company title scheme	Strata scheme	Rental
Entry fee	Lump sum	Lump sum	Lump sum	Lump sum	Rent
Cooling-off period	7 business days	7 business days	7 business days	7 business days	7 business days
Change of mind after moving in (settling-in period)	90 days	90 days	90 days	90 days	90 days
Ongoing					
Service fees	Yes	Yes	Yes	Yes, plus strata fees	Yes (may be included in rent)
Sinking fund fee	Included in service fee	Included in service fee	Included in service fee	Included in service fee or strata fees	No
Cap on increases to service fees Exceptions may apply (e.g. new services or facilities)	CPI	CPI	CPI	CPI (plus strata fee increases)	Rent increases as per contract

	Lease (registered interest holder)	Lease/ licence (non-registered interest holder)	Company title scheme	Strata scheme	Rental
Outgoing					
Service fees after leaving	42 days	42 days	Until property is sold	Until property is sold	No
Exit fee	Yes	Yes	Yes	Yes	No
Reinstatement/ refurbishment costs	Resident damage only	Resident damage only	Yes	Yes	Resident damage only
Marketing costs **Residents must pay their own real estate agent's costs**	Shared as per capital gain	Operator	Resident	Resident	No
Capital gain when property sold	50% or more to resident	Lease – 50% or more to operator Licence – as per contract	Resident	Resident	Operator
Risk of loss on sale of property	As per contract	As per contract	Resident	Resident	Operator

	Lease (registered interest holder)	Lease/ licence (non-registered interest holder)	Company title scheme	Strata scheme	Rental
Guaranteed buyback	No	6 months	No	No	N/A
Willable asset Exit entitlement or sale proceeds (if any) can be gifted	No	No	No	No	No

TABLE 12: Summary of rights, responsibilities and costs in land lease communities, under the Residential (Land Lease) Communities Act 2013 (NSW)

	Land lease (own the house, lease the land)		Rental (rent both the house and the land)
	House	Land	
Age restriction	Designed for 'over 55s'		
Right to occupy	Permanent	Permanent	Temporary
Maximum or typical term of contract	Until house is sold	Until house is sold	As per contract
Ownership of property/ title registration	Resident	Operator	Operator
Ingoing			
Stamp duty	No	No	No
Deposit	Yes	No	Bond required
Deposit refund	As per contract	N/A	Yes
Minimum time to consider documents	No	14 days	No
Contracts to sign	Contract to buy house	Lease over the land	Rental agreement
Entry fee	Purchase price	No	Bond + two weeks rent in advance
Cooling-off period	No	14 days	No

	Land lease (own the house, lease the land)		Rental (rent both the house and the land)
	House	Land	
Ongoing			
Lease fees	N/A	Site fees set by operator (formula for increases specified)	Weekly rent subject to operator increases
Outgoing			
Lease fees after leaving	N/A	Yes	N/A
Exit fee	N/A	Most don't, but some do	No
Refurbishment	Yes, at resident's discretion	N/A	No
Marketing costs and sales commissions	Yes, residents must pay their own real estate agent's costs	No	No
Capital gain when property sold	Yes	N/A	N/A
Risk of loss on sale of property	Resident	N/A	N/A
Guaranteed buyback	No	N/A	N/A
Willable asset	Transferrable	Yes, if there is an exit fee, this is normally payable on transfer	No

From the developer's perspective

So you can appreciate both sides of the picture, let's now look at it from the developers' point of view.

Developers are in business to make a profit; but operating a retirement community is very different from building a strata development. If they are looking to establish and maintain a thriving business, they will be trying to give the best service possible. This entails building a house, townhouse or apartment that is value for money in its price range, and then providing good ongoing service via the management of the village.

The problem with building retirement communities is that they contain far more than just homes to live in. There is normally an administration block, security fencing and recreational amenities such as a lounge, pool and tennis court. The bigger the complex the more opportunities there are to save money because of economies of scale but, as the complex gets bigger, more capital is required to build it.

If the developers build a large retirement community in stages, they have to build many of the common facilities at the start. This places a huge cost burden on the first units sold, as they are carrying the bulk of the infrastructure costs for the entire project. So in the early stages, the developer is often not making a profit.

In retirement villages, the operators are prohibited from making a profit on the general service charge of the village; their profit comes from the exit fee. The general service charges are much like a body corporate: they cover the cost of running the village, and residents can have input into the budget. These rules don't apply to LLCs. LLC operators can and often do profit from their site fees — site fees are often higher than the general service charges of a retirement village, but this is offset by lower exit fees or none at all.

Reputable developers build retirement communities with a long term attitude. They realise that if they build a quality product it may not be possible to recover their costs in the early stages. They build in the expectation that a good reputation will ensure strong sales and in the later stages they will make a profit.

Legislative protections

For leasehold and licence retirement villages, legislation includes some important consumer protection provisions.

1. **Security of tenure:** Legislation limits the circumstances in which a retirement village operator can require a resident to leave. In some situations, the resident's right to occupy ranks ahead of any mortgage registered over the village land.

2. **Statutory charge:** Legislation generally gives the resident security that they will be repaid the refundable part of their entry payment. This is achieved through a statutory charge, which is similar to a mortgage over residential land.

3. **Limits on increases to service charges:** Legislation often limits increases to the service charge paid by a resident — generally to CPI — unless a majority of residents approve a higher increase.

4. **Special levies:** Freehold villages are also regulated by state-based strata laws in addition to the retirement villages legislation. Under strata laws residents can be

required to meet special levies for capital works and building defects, whereas residents who are on a lease-hold or licence contract generally are not responsible for these costs.

Alternative contracts

In the church, charity and not-for-profit sector (the original providers of retirement villages) there have long been different payment options offered — in some cases the payment arrangement was (and potentially still is) tailored to the individual resident, while in other cases the operator may offer the same unit on two, three or even seven different payment arrangements. Big operators, such as Bolton Clarke (who have 39 villages nationally) and Baptist Care, who recently merged their NSW and WA villages, as well as many smaller operators offer alternative payment options — and these are not always advertised. So it can pay to ask if the village you want to move to can offer something other than their standard options, so that you can afford to move there.

In the for-profit sector, for a long time the standard model was a 30% DMF over 10 years: simply 3% per year. In recent times, the most common DMF is still 30% but the length of time it accumulates over is shorter, typically five or six years. Around three-quarters of the industry now base their DMF on the purchase price, others are based on the resale price. In the last few years, three of the biggest for-profit operators — Levande (formerly Stockland), Aveo and Keyton (formerly Lendlease) — have introduced alternative contracts … and they are all different.

IRT: Sliding scales

IRT (previously known as Illawarra Retirement Trust) is a non-profit operator of 31 villages across New South Wales, Australian Capital Territory and Queensland. They offer prospective residents up to four different payment options. These range from a donation (you pay around half the full price, but it is all a donation to the organisation) through to an option with no deferred management fee (DMF), so you get back the entire amount you pay. In the middle is a typical DMF of 30% and a lower DMF option of 15%. Basically, it is a sliding scale: the more you pay upfront the less you pay at the end. IRT also have a rental option for people who are financially disadvantaged.

Aveo: Pay your management fee now, later or not at all

Aveo offers three contract options called "Now", "Later" and "Bond".

Of all the different payment options in the market, theirs is probably the simplest to understand — basically it's up to you whether you pay your management fee now, later, or not at all. There are a number of financial terms standard across all the contracts: management fees are based on the purchase price, no sharing in capital gain or loss, no marketing fees or sales commissions and no renovation costs. There is also a six-month move-in guarantee: if you move to a village and move out within the first six months they give you your money back.

As we explained earlier, retirement villages can't profit from ongoing fees: the contracts are really about how much you pay when you move in and how much you get back (and how quickly) after you leave.

The Later option is a typical retirement village contract, you pay the lowest price upfront with a 35% deferred management fee at the end, and a buyback guarantee of six months.

The Now option lets you pay a management fee of 20% now, instead of 35% later. The fee is amortised over two years, so if you only live in the village for a year then 5% is refunded to you. Like the Later option, there is a six-month buyback guarantee.

The Bond option increases the purchase price by 40% and also has an establishment fee of 3%, which is not refundable. Under this contract you get your entire purchase price back, with a buyback guarantee of three months.

TABLE 13: *Summary of Aveo contract options*

	Aveo retirement villages		
	Now	**Later**	**Bond**
Ingoing			
Purchase price	Standard price + 20% management fee	Standard price	Standard price + 40% + non-refundable 3% establishment fee
Ongoing			
Service fee	Weekly/monthly service fee is the same for all contracts		

	Aveo retirement villages		
	Now	Later	Bond
Outgoing			
DMF	The 20% management fee is amortised over 2 years, you get back the standard price	The DMF is 35% accrued over 3 years	You get back the standard price + 40% in full
Capital gain/loss	No	No	No
Refurbishment costs	No	No	No
Selling fees	No	No	No
Moving-in guarantee	6 months	6 months	6 months
Buyback guarantee	6 months	6 months	3 months
Move with ease	Transfer to another Aveo village and receive a credit for any management fee already paid in your current village		

Across their more than 90 villages, the Later price (which is often the referenced price when comparing it to other villages as that is the one that has an exit fee) varies from $95,000 to $4.5 million, although most prices tend to be around $500,000.

Let's put the payment options into a real-life context.

CASE STUDY — Terry

Terry is downsizing from his home worth $750,000; he has $200,000 of investments and $10,000 of personal assets. He is moving into an Aveo village where the 2-bedroom apartment he is looking at can be purchased under any of the three prices:

- *$500,000 if he pays his management fee later*
- *$600,000 if he pays his management fee now or*
- *$721,000 if he chooses the bond contract.*

Let's look at what those payment options mean for Terry.

	Now	Later	Bond
Ingoing			
Purchase price	$600,000	$600,000	$700,000
Establishment fee	–	–	$21,000
Investments	$450,000	$350,000	$250,000
Personal assets	$10,000	$10,000	$10,000
Ongoing			
General service charge	$7,200	$7,200	$7,200
Personal expenses	$26,000	$26,000	$26,000
Age pension	$16,171	$23,971	$28,514
Investment income @ 4% p.a.	$18,000	$14,000	$10,000

	Now	Later	Bond
Outgoing			
After 1 year	$425,000	$550,000	$700,000
After 2 years	$375,000	$500,000	$700,000
After 5 years	$325,000	$500,000	$700,000
After 10 years	$325,000	$500,000	$700,000
Guaranteed buyback	6 months	6 months	3 months

Keyton (formerly Lendlease Retirement): Flexibility for your circumstances

Keyton has the most dynamic contract alternatives in the for-profit sector. In most of their leasehold villages, they offer four payment options, which span from a rental-style "pay as you go" option to a fully refundable contribution. The payment options have lots of moving parts, altering not just the amount you pay on entry and on exit, but in the case of the pay as you go option, the amount you pay along the way and how quickly you receive the funds after you leave the village.

It's a bit like being able to move a slider on whichever cost is most important to you, then have all the sliders on the other costs adjust automatically.

TABLE 14: Summary of Keyton contract options

	Standard (DMF)	Prepaid plan	Refundable contribution	Pay as you go
Ingoing				
Purchase price	Purchase price	Purchase price + 19%	Purchase price + 30%	No
Establishment fee (non-refundable)	No	No	3.5% of purchase price	3 months of monthly payment
Security deposit (refundable in whole or part)	No	No	No	24 months of monthly payment (independent Living Units) OR 3 months of monthly payments (Serviced Apartments)
Ongoing				
Service fee	Weekly/ monthly	Weekly/ monthly	Weekly/ monthly	Weekly/ monthly
Monthly payment	No	No	No	0.5% of purchase price

	Standard (DMF)	Prepaid plan	Refundable contribution	Pay as you go
Outgoing				
DMF	32% of sale price	No	No	No
Long term maintenance fund	4% of resale price	No	No	No
Capital gain/loss	100%	100%	No	No
Refurbishment costs	Yes	Yes	No	No
Selling costs	Yes	Yes	No	No
Guaranteed buyback/refund	Paid on settlement or after legislated buyback period	Paid on settlement or after legislated buyback period	Paid 60 days after exit	Paid 60 days after exit

From your point of view, there are some key reasons why one payment option may suit you better than another. For example, you may not want (or be able) to sell your current home, in which case a model that doesn't require you to outlay as much capital, such as the "Standard" contract, may appeal. Many people view the move to a retirement community as an opportunity to free up some of the capital in the family home and either invest those funds to fund the lifestyle they desire or use the money to purchase lifestyle assets such as a boat or caravan — or perhaps you plan to do both.

Of course, if you receive a pension, you need to factor any change to your entitlement into such a plan. People who are concerned about the loss of pension that can come with downsizing may find a contract where they can pay more now and less later more attractive — after all, as we pointed out earlier, the loss of pension at $7,800 per year for every $100,000 over the asset test threshold can be tough. A contract like the "Refundable Contribution" option could mean that paying, say, an extra $200,000 now (with little or no exit fee later) maintains your pension at $15,600/year more. If you live in the village for 10 years, the combination of the reduced (or zero) exit fee and the increase in pension could be worth hundreds of thousands. For others, it won't be so much about money as terms and conditions. Contracts that provide certainty through guaranteed buybacks, settling-in guarantees and no selling fees are becoming more popular — of course to get this level of certainty often means you are giving up any capital gain.

Fixed price exit fee with LDK Healthcare

The industry norm for deferred management fees has always been to take a percentage of either the upfront purchase price or the outgoing sale price. But one group, LDK Seniors Living, has entered the market with a fixed price DMF — they call it a membership fee — which you can choose to pay at the start, or at the end.

At Greenway Views in Canberra, if you choose to pay on entry it costs $265,000; and if you pay on exit it is $340,000.

The membership fee is calculated on a pro-rata basis for the first three years. In the first year, residents will accrue 50% of their membership fee. In the second and third year residents accrue 25% of their village membership fee. For example, if you chose to pay upfront and leave the village after one year then your membership fee would be $132,500 and the remaining $132,500 would be refunded to you with your exit entitlement. Your exit entitlement is what you paid for your unit: there is no capital gain or capital loss, the operator meets any refurbishment fees and selling costs, and guarantees buyback within six months.

While you live in the village, the general service charge you pay is fixed for life, which means, on the one hand, certainty of costs for each person, and on the other, residents paying different prices for the same services, based on when they moved in. Meals and care delivered by the village are charged at cost.

TABLE 15: LDK Healthcare membership options

	Pay on entry	Pay on exit
Ingoing		
Purchase price	$745,000–$1,400,000	$745,000–$1,400,000
Membership fee	$265,000	No
Ongoing		
General service charge (fixed for life and includes utilities)	$295/week	$295/week

	Pay on entry	Pay on exit
Outgoing		
Exit fee	No	$340,000 membership fee
Other costs	No capital gain/loss, No refurbishment cost, No marketing or selling fees	
Guaranteed buyback	6 months	

A fixed exit fee is certainly a different option, and one that could represent significant savings, especially at the higher prices. A $1,400,000 apartment on a 30% exit fee would be $420,000 compared with $340,000 on a fixed price when you leave, or better still $265,000 upfront — a saving of $75,000 (as a percentage it is just under 19%). On the lower priced apartments the membership fee would be higher if you look at it in percentage terms. An $800,000 apartment where you pay upfront is equivalent to a 33% management fee, and if you pay at the end it is equivalent to 42.5%.

For people who receive the age pension, having a fixed price exit fee can remove one of the key drawbacks of purchasing a more expensive unit (which can be a worthwhile strategy to increase or maintain pension entitlement), which is that is that the exit fee goes up too. It's certainly worth crunching the numbers.

Graeme @ GemLife, Woodend

I really like the community feel.

I was living in Melbourne in a 2-bed, 1-bath apartment in Kensington, and I saw an ad on the internet that there was an over-55's living place being built in Woodend by GemLife. I made a phone call, and that, as they say, is that. I went and had a look at an open day: there were four houses open for inspection, so I had a look at each one, decided on this one and put a deposit down.

Then Covid hit.

I sold my apartment in Melbourne and was able to marry up settlement with moving into this one, which was good. I moved in a week before Christmas 2020, and had the family over to my place on Christmas Day.

I wanted to downsize; I wanted to get out of the city, but I had no intention of looking for a stand-alone home. I was born in the country, so I was always keen to go back. In fact, 35 years earlier a mate and I had a house in Woodend. I moved from a 2-bed, 1-bath apartment of about 19 m^2 to a 3-bed, 2-bath home of 28 m^2 with a double garage, so I didn't downsize, I upsized.

It's great to be part of the community. I'm single and I still work — lots of other people here are single, and quite a few others in the community also work. At the moment there are 25 or 30 homes that are empty because a lot of people live here so that they can lock and leave to travel interstate or overseas.

I really like the community feel. You can get involved in as much or as little as you like. If you want a bit of quiet you can hibernate in your home. But if you want to get out there's literally a smorgasboard of things to do. We have a clubhouse that has a lounge and dining area and outside it has chess, tennis, petanque and BBQs. There's a pool, spa and sauna, two bowling alleys, a theatrette that's like going to gold class, a six-ring undercover bowls lawn, a craft shop, and a men's shed. I get involved in the men's shed — we have all the tools we need to make or assemble things. I'm planning on putting a veggie pod in my backyard when I retire.

I'm slowly transitioning to retirement; I'm down to three days a week now, then it will be two. It will give me time to do other things — like drive around in my old MG. I come from a sporting background (I played AFL for Carlton and Richmond) I still like to play golf, go for walks, ride my bike, there's a few groups here that enjoying doing those things. I enjoy cooking too: there's a group of us who go to each other's place for dinner, or we might have four or five people over for morning tea. My family are on this side of town, so I'm on the right side to visit them too.

The bar in the clubhouse is open Thursday to Sunday, and whenever there is a special event on. You can pay cash or card, and buy wine by the glass or bottle — it's much cheaper than going out to a hotel.

We have a residents committee that organises different events, like a few weeks ago we had an ABBA night, and from time to time there are special guest speakers ... there's regular raffles and meat trays, and money raised from the bar comes back into the community.

We have a village bus — a 20-seat Mercedes Benz — that takes us on outings. I haven't been, but I know it's made trips to Bendigo, Ballarat and Melbourne to visit art shows, the theatre, and a fancy high tea. GemLife don't organise it: the residents oragnise it themselves, but the bus takes them.

The biggest surprise for me has been how easy it is to keep my new home clean. It takes no time: a quick vacuum and I do the bathrooms, it's all low maintenance, and it's good as new.

I think if I had my time over I would have culled more of my stuff: I've brought a lot of things that I really don't them anymore. The furniture I had just didn't work, it didn't match this house and as this place is much bigger than my old one I bought a big television and new couches to match the new house and enjoy all my extra space. I have really enjoyed making it what I want: choosing the furniture and the pictures for the walls and the like. My advice would be to cull before you move, look at your new home, and organise what you need and what suits your new home.

PART 3:

AND WHEN YOU NEED MORE SUPPORT?

Most people firmly announce that when they need care it will be home delivered — as though it's Uber Eats. The government do a great job of affirming this way of thinking, with their rhetoric about home care, but the reality can be quite different to the headlines. Sadly, anyone who has navigated getting home care for themselves or a loved one will tell you that it can be a nightmare.

In November 2019, as part of its response to the Royal Commission into Aged Care Quality and Safety's Interim Report, the Albanese Government announced its intention to create a single in-home care program. The new Support at Home program is expected to provide support to more than one million senior Australians and will replace four programs: the Commonwealth Home Support Programme (CHSP), Home Care Packages Program, Short Term Restorative Care Program and Transitional Care Program. Support at Home's aim is to deliver timely and flexible care services that are tailored to people's needs. The program was due to begin on 1 July 2023, but has been pushed back to 1 July 2024 to enable better design and industry preparation for the new program.

In this part, we'll cover what services are available now, and how you get access to them.

12

ENTRY-LEVEL SUPPORT

The options for basic help at home are currently the Commonwealth Home Support Programme (CHSP), or the Veterans' Home Care (VHC) and Community Nursing Programmes. These programs provide simple support for people with straightforward needs.

You can also start by accessing privately funded care, if you have the means to do so.

Commonwealth Home Support Programme (CHSP)

CHSP is designed to provide the most basic level of support and care — services available within CHSP include: personal care, such as showering and dressing; domestic assistance, such as preparation of meals, assistance with laundry, shopping, housework and gardening; transport to social activities or doctors' appointments; and providing meals, such as Meals on Wheels, an incredibly popular CHSP service.

CHSP may also provide assistance with housing for people who are at risk of homelessness.

To access CHSP you will need to have your care needs assessed and meet the age requirements, which is generally over the age of 65 (or over 50 for Aboriginal and Torres Strait Islander people). However, if you have a low income, are homeless or at risk of being homeless this age restriction is reduced to 50 (or 45 years for Aboriginal and Torres Strait Islander people).

First you need an initial telephone assessment with the My Aged Care contact centre, normally followed up with a face-to-face appointment with the Regional Assessment Service (RAS).

The amount you pay for CHSP services varies from one provider to another and from one individual to another, based on a pricing framework set by government, which providers use to tier their pricing for people with different levels of income. Because of the variations, you should confirm the cost before you start receiving any service — below is a table showing what costs *may* look like.

Meals on Wheels provide support to around 200,000 people every year through a workforce of 45,000 volunteers.
Source: Canterbury Meals on Wheels, Campsie

TABLE 16: *CHSP pricing examples*

CHSP service	Pensioner	Part pensioner	Self-funded
	Rate per hour (unless otherwise specified)		
Domestic assistance	$15.00	$22.00	$60.00
Personal care	$15.00	$22.00	$60.00
Home maintenance	$16.30	$22.25	$58.50
Day therapy	$11.50	$11.50	$11.50
Home respite	$6.35	$10.35	$36.60
Delivered meals	$8.70 per meal	$12.40 per meal	$16.55 per meal
Assisted transport	$6.25 each way	$10.15 each way	$36.00 each way
Community bus	$3.40 each way	$5.60 each way	$7.90 each way

As you can see, with this pricing, self-funded retirees may be better off buying some services directly.

The services you can access through CHSP will depend on your provider. Generally, they are not as flexible as a home care package. The provider coordinates the services and who provides them, so you may have limited flexibility in the day and time that any service is provided, as the provider tries to manage their roster, and naturally the amount of care you can receive will be limited based on their resources.

Almost everyone (98% of people) assessed as eligible for a home care package was also assessed as eligible for CHSP. And some more good news: wait times to start a CHSP tend to be measured in weeks, rather than months.

Veterans' Home Care (VHC) and Community Nursing Programmes

In addition to other home care services, the Australian Government through the Department of Veterans' Affairs (DVA) offers a range of services for veterans and their war widows/widowers.

To be eligible to receive VHC services you must have a Gold or White Repatriation Health Card. There may still be limits and restrictions on the amount and type of services different veterans can access, so it is best to check what is available to you with DVA.

VHC packages are designed to help people with low care needs. They can include personal care, domestic assistance, short term social assistance, safety-related home and garden maintenance, and respite care. If you are eligible for VHC, you can still receive services through other government-funded programs, such as CHSP or home care packages, as well as short term care services (as long as there is no doubling up of the services provided).

Services received through other programs are charged at the rate applicable to the particular service provider, and VHC clients may find they are better off with VHC rates. A small co-payment is normally required and there is a limit both to the amount you will pay, and to the amount of the service you can access.

TABLE 17: *VHC co-payment arrangements, at 1 July 2023*

	Rate	Maximum cost	Maximum service
Personal care	$5/hour	$5/week	1 hour 30 minutes/week
Domestic assistance	$5/hour	$10/week	Based on assessment
Home and garden maintenance	$5/hour	$75/year	15 hours/year
Respite services	No co-payment applies	N/A	196 hours in-home *or* 28 days in residential care *or* a combination
Emergency short term home relief (ESTHR)	No co-payment applies	N/A	Up to 216 hours per financial year

People who cannot afford the co-payment can apply to DVA to waive their fees.

The assessment for VHC packages is conducted by the regional VHC assessment agency. You can be referred to this service by your doctor or other medical professional or you can arrange the assessment yourself.

If you are eligible for DVA services but require more care than can be provided through VHC, you may be referred to the DVA Community Nursing Program, which will coordinate a care plan for you. This program provides clinical nursing and personal care services, such as help with medication, wound care, hygiene and showering or dressing to eligible veterans and war widow/ers in their own homes. There is no co-payment for DVA Community Nursing Programme.

Private care

Long wait times, expensive margins and limited access to care through CHSP, home care packages and other programs has created huge demand for private home care services. You can set up a relationship with a private care provider with no delay, as you do not need an assessment. When you just need a bit of help, or are waiting for a home care package, private care can be set up fast and need not break the bank. Once you start getting your home care package you may find that you still need some private care to "top up" your funded care to give you all of the care you need.

Services available through private care providers vary from one provider to another, and so does the cost. Generally speaking, the service, level of qualifications, time of day and day of the week will be key factors in determining the price. Services that require no formal qualifications — such as meal preparation, coordinating activities such as crafts, collecting prescriptions/groceries and housekeeping — are significantly cheaper than services that require nursing supervision — such as assistance with changing dressings or administering medications. You will typically find the lowest prices for services between 8am and 4pm Monday to Friday. Beyond these hours the cost goes up, and if you want a service on a Sunday night or a public holiday don't be surprised if the price is more than triple.

In some circumstances, your private care may come from the same provider as your home care package or CHSP service. If so, discuss the total package of services with them and let them build a care plan around your needs and the services for which you can get funding.

We have also seen a number of situations where people decided to continue with private care at home as their needs increased. And that decision was right for those people — but costs were generally over $150,000 per year. Even with the highest level of home care package to offset costs, they were still looking at out of pocket expenses of over $100,000 for the amount of care needed. And that's just for the care: you still need to add to that your cost of living — meals, activities, medication etc.

Sometimes it is really about how important it is for you to stay in your home. And sometimes, as we've shown in this book, people who initially assumed that staying at home was essential have discovered other options that made them much happier. Things that were once a joy can become a burden. Many people assume that moving into residential aged care will be cheaper than topping up a home care package, but — particularly for self-funded retirees — that is not necessarily the case.

If your care needs are such that you are thinking about an aged care facility, the costs vary widely. The average RAD price across the country is around $450,000 at the moment, and if you pay that by daily payment it will cost $36,675 year. On top of that you have the basic daily fee (which everyone pays) of $22,214 per year, plus any additional or extra services, and then the means-tested care fee of up to $32,719 per year (with a lifetime cap of $78,525).

So for a self-funded retiree, a move to residential aged care could easily cost somewhere between $90,000 and a bit more than $100,000 a year. But if you stay in aged care for a couple of years or more (or if you have contributed to the cost of a home care package through an income-tested care fee) the lifetime cap will kick in and your means-tested care fee will reduce to $0 — saving you $32,719 per year from then on.

Let's look at how you can get started with other care options.

13

YOUR ACAT ASSESSMENT

To be eligible to receive a number of government funded care services you need an assessment by an Aged Care Assessment Team (usually just referred to as an ACAT).

"ACAT" is a term you will come across repeatedly if you are investigating aged care services. ACAT means Aged Care Assessment Team; in Victoria, it is "ACAS" (for Aged Care Assessment Service). We will use ACAT to mean both.

ACAT assessments are free and will normally be carried out in your home, although sometimes they are conducted within a hospital. Most people are referred to the ACAT by their doctor, community nurse or social worker but you — or a family member — can make direct contact with the ACAT yourself, through My Aged Care. Rest assured that the ACAT interview process is a relatively easy one and the team's objective is to help you.

The ACAT can approve you to receive:

- a home care package
- short term restorative care
- a transitional care program
- respite in an aged care facility
- permanent entry to an aged care facility
  or a combination of these services.

Don't delay

Unfortunately, many people put off applying for a home care package because they read headlines like "10,000 extra home care packages", and feel reassured that when the time comes that they really need help, there will be plenty of packages available. Typical excuses for delay include, "I don't really need it yet," "Other people need it more than I do," and, "I don't want strangers coming into my house".

First, depending on where you live and how busy your local ACAT team are, getting your assessment can take anything from a few weeks to a few months. Second, if the assessment approves you for a home care package, you join the national prioritisation queue to receive a package. We explain more about this below, but the latest figures at time of writing show that there are around 31,000 people waiting for a home care package at their approved level. The average waiting time for someone given medium priority is between one and three months, across all package levels, however there have been cases of people waiting more than a year. So applying for a home care package won't result in a carer on your doorstep next Monday — it might not even result in care this year! Don't delay.

What happens in the assessment?

The ACAT is a team of people that includes doctors, nurses, social workers and therapists. In most cases you will have contact with one or two people only. The assessment is very straightforward: just a chat about your day-to-day activities, the things you are comfortable doing for yourself and the things you may need assistance with. These questions could range from how easily you are coping with showering or dressing to whether you have difficulties carrying the shopping home. They will also ask about your general health, and may request a copy of your medical history from your doctor. During this meeting you will be asked to express your ideas about your care needs and which services you think would be of help.

A common mistake people make during their ACAT assessment is focusing on a particular service that meets their care needs today. For example, people currently living at home often only want the ACAT to approve them for a home care package. But respite in an aged care facility may be wanted or needed at some time in the future — if you are ever contemplating moving into a residential aged care facility then respite is a great way to try before you buy. If you are approved for respite, your assessment will designate your care needs as either low or high. For permanent entry to an aged care facility, the assessment will simply say that you are approved for these services.

If you don't get approval for such services now, you will need to request another assessment when you do want them. And you'll be up for another wait for the new assessment.

The information shared in the assessment meeting will be used to determine your care needs, and which care service/s will be best for you. You will get written confirmation of the outcome of your assessment, including why the ACAT made their decisions, and which services you have been approved for, in a document called a "support plan", but often referred to as your "ACAT assessment" or "ACAT approval". They will also provide you with information about service providers in your area.

Having approval for different services doesn't mean you need to use them. In many cases, there is a waiting list. Think of your ACAT approval like having a passport: if you need to travel overseas, you have the document that enables you to do so.

Like a passport, it's important to *keep* your ACAT support plan: each approved service has a referral code that you need to give the provider to confirm that you are eligible for their services. It will remain valid indefinitely unless it has a time restriction applied to it. If it does, and expires, you will need to be re-assessed.

Not happy?

The idea of being assessed by a stranger or group of strangers can be very daunting. Knowing your rights, and what will happen when and why, can help reduce your anxiety. It is also a good idea to have a family member, carer or friend present — if you wish, you can have an independent advocate attend the assessment with you. Of course, if you need an interpreter you can bring one or the ACAT can arrange to have one in attendance.

If you are unhappy with your assessment you should discuss any concerns with the person in charge of the ACAT Team. If the assessment determines that you are not eligible to receive aged care services, or you need to escalate your issue, you can lodge an appeal.

Now you wait

Your support plan will specify the assistance you are eligible to receive. But you may not be able to get hold of it right away. For home care packages you join the national prioritisation queue.

We are not telling you this to discourage from seeking a home care package: quite the opposite. If staying at home is what you really want, you need to plan for that — once again the old adage that "failing to plan is planning to fail" is true.

14

HOME CARE PACKAGES

Home care packages are designed to support people with higher care needs than CHSP — although whether you get more or less care through a home care package will depend on the level of package you receive, and the cost of administration and other fees, as well as the services in your package.

There are four levels of home care packages:

- **Home Care Level 1** — to support people with basic care needs.
- **Home Care Level 2** — to support people with low level care needs.
- **Home Care Level 3** — to support people with intermediate care needs.
- **Home Care Level 4** — to support people with high care needs.

Just like CHSP, your package can include a range of services covering assistance with personal care, such as showering and dressing; domestic assistance, such as preparation of meals, assistance with laundry, shopping, housework and gardening; and transport to social activities or doctors' appointments. It can also include home modifications, access to technology, and aids and appliances. When it comes to home care packages, the services you access and who provides them is up to you — this is the key difference between CHSP and home care packages.

Once you have ACAT approval for a home care package, you wait in the national prioritisation queue for a home care package to become available. When it's your turn, the package that is available may not be at your assessed level, for example, you may have been approved for a level 3 package, but what's available is a level 2 package. In that case, you can take the level 2 package as an "interim package" and remain in the queue until it is your turn to receive a level 3 package, or you can turn down the interim package and continue to wait for a package at your level.

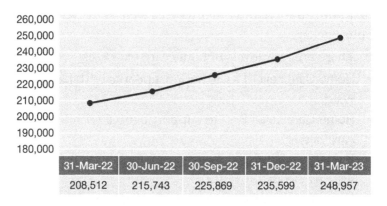

	31-Mar-22	30-Jun-22	30-Sep-22	31-Dec-22	31-Mar-23
	208,512	215,743	225,869	235,599	248,957

Number of people with a home care package since 31 March 2023

At 31 March 2023, almost 269,000 people had access to a home care package, that's an 18% increase (41,535 people) from March 2022. At the same time there were about 31,000 people waiting for a home care package: about 24,000 people were waiting without any package, while about 7,000 were waiting with an interim package at a lower level.

TABLE 18: Numbers and percentages of people with a home care package at 31 March 2023

State/territory	Level 1	Level 2	Level 3	Level 4	Total	Share
NSW	6,713	36,610	27,070	13,327	83,720	33.6%
VIC	3,242	29,374	19,886	14,480	66,982	26.9%
QLD	2,073	17,899	16,713	10,613	47,298	19.0%
WA	262	4,711	6,854	7,675	19,502	7.8%
SA	744	7,626	8,717	4,832	21,919	8.8%
TAS	250	2,131	2,210	1,143	5,734	2.3%
ACT	33	855	801	961	2,650	1.1%
NT	3	400	398	345	1,146	0.5%
Unknown	0	3	0	3	6	0.0%
Total	13,320	99,609	82,649	53,379	248,957	100.0%
Share	5.4%	40.0%	33.2%	21.4%	100.0%	

TABLE 19: *Number of people waiting on a home care package at their approved level by state and territory of residence and level of approval at 31 March 2023*

State/territory	Level 1	Level 2	Level 3	Level 4	Total	Share
NSW	503	3,600	4,971	1,563	**10,637**	**34.5%**
VIC	254	2,716	3,489	1,319	**7,778**	**25.2%**
QLD	200	1,977	2,396	760	**5,333**	**17.3%**
WA	29	511	1,380	763	**2,683**	**8.7%**
SA	64	859	1,510	565	**2,998**	**9.7%**
TAS	18	285	419	162	**884**	**2.9%**
ACT	2	93	152	61	**308**	**1.0%**
NT	–	49	103	38	**190**	**0.6%**
Unknown	3	10	14	1	**28**	**0.1%**
Total	**1,073**	**10,100**	**14,434**	**5,232**	**30,839**	**100.0%**
Share	**3.5%**	**32.8%**	**46.8%**	**17.0%**	**100.0%**	

Anyone who has tried to navigate home care for themselves or a loved one will tell you that it seems to be a test of patience, resourcefulness and forensic accounting. You need patience while you wait for assessment and then for care to start; resourcefulness in finding services, volunteers and family members to fill in the gaps; and forensic accounting to determine whether or not you are getting bang for your buck.

But hang in there. Once you get the system working for you, it can make all the difference to your quality of life.

David: Life after stroke

As part of my package I got taxi vouchers, which gave me my independence again. It's made a huge difference: it gives me the ability to make choices for myself.

I was involved in basketball initially, working as a chiropractor and so I got the basketball work and then word spread, and other clients started coming. In the end I practised for over 40 years.

David and his wife Doris

But I had a stroke in 2007. The doctor came in and told my boys that they did not know if I would make it through the night. They couldn't say if I would walk again. I was in rehab for six months. I said: "I'm not leaving here unless I can walk out the door". I asked my three-year-old granddaughter, "Will you help me walk out the door?" and she held my hand

and had a smile from ear to ear as we walked out of the hospital together.

I tried to go back to work. Doris, my wife, didn't think that seemed right — the doctors said I could, so I tried ... but it just wasn't working, so we sold the business.

After the stroke I felt that I had to get back into service. I was always involved in community service. One of the best things was getting involved with the Boroondara stroke support group, who run a number of programs. They had a lawn bowls club, and when I went along I realised I missed the competition of sport. Winning or losing is not all-important, but in the moment I need to help the team win, then I need to win.

Before the stroke I was quite involved in Life Education and Rotary, but I drifted away from them because I just couldn't get to the meetings. Life Education is a drug education program for primary school children run out of mobile learning centres. The presenters teach about the effects that drugs can have on children. We also teach that it's ok to say no, and it's ok for your friends to say no.

Recently I was presented an honorary life award from Life Education in recognition of my commitment to the organisation. One of the caravans we use for school visits was named after me, and I was delighted to have that caravan visit my granddaughters' school, as she was thrilled to see the plaque on the caravan.

I found out about home care packages through a friend who was getting one. It was five years after my stroke. All I wanted was to take pressure off Doris — with my drivers licence being cancelled immediately after the stroke, I was relying on Doris a lot.

As part of my package I got taxi vouchers, which gave me my independence again. It's made a huge difference: it gives me the ability to make choices for myself.

My home care package also provides things I used to pay for out of my own pocket, such as podiatry, hearing aids, glasses, and my gym membership. Plus I get some window cleaning and heavy gardening done a couple of times a year.

My home care package provider is terrific. They are always there to answer questions — I'm not just a number at the end of the phone. They give me great advice about how I can use my funds to help with day-to-day things.

I used to say to people — I was a mentor to new stroke sufferers — "Don't do what so many people have done, and ask 'Why me?' It's a question with no answer. It's happened to you, and you've got to get off your bum and deal with it. That's why I've stayed so involved. I don't want to sit around. Be involved — be useful — it helps to fill in time, and you know that you are doing something positive."

Costs of home care packages

Everyone who receives a home care package can be asked to pay a basic daily fee, though this is negotiable, if you cannot afford to pay it. The maximum contribution is based on the level of your package, with the highest rate being equal to 17.5% of the age pension — currently $12.53 per day.

TABLE 20: Home care package maximum basic daily fees, at 20 September 2023

Home care package	Basic daily fee
Home Care Level 1	$11.22
Home Care Level 2	$11.87
Home Care Level 3	$12.20
Home Care Level 4	$12.53

Your ability to contribute more than the basic daily fee is assessed on your income. Full pensioners do not pay an income-tested care fee. People with higher levels of income, based on Centrelink's income test for the age pension, will pay an income-tested care fee.

Once your income exceeds the threshold (pension plus allowed income) you will need to pay a contribution towards your cost of care at 50c/dollar. The income-tested care fee is capped at $6,544/year for people with the same income as a part pensioner, and $13,087/year for self-funded retirees. There is also a lifetime cap of $78,525 that first applies to the income-tested care fee and later, if you move into residential aged care, to the means-tested care fee.

For example, if you receive a home care package for three years, and pay $20,000 of income-tested fees towards your home care package in that time, when you move into residential aged care you will pay means-tested care fees up to $58,525, at which point you have reached the lifetime limit of $78,525 and no further means-tested fees will apply. Because the means-tested care fees have an annual cap of $32,719, you can pay up to that cap in the first year and then in the second year once you have paid $25,806 you will have reached the lifetime cap. Of course these fees get indexed so the actual amounts increase each year in line with the indexation.

What is more, your income-tested fee cannot exceed the cost of your care — which is the funding the government provide.

Calculating how much income-tested care fee you will be charged is the role of Centrelink (or DVA if you receive a pension through them). They will use their income test — which may be very different to the actual income you receive. There is also an option to be "means not disclosed", in which case you just pay the maximum income-tested care fee of $36/day. You are still eligible for the annual cap and lifetime limit. As a general rule, if you are a pensioner you will be better off disclosing, but if you are a self-funded retiree you might as well estimate your liability before filling in the form — after all, if you are going to pay the maximum amount either way then you can save yourself the time and hassle of completing the paperwork.

As a guide, to reach the maximum income-tested care fee you would need to have annual income of around $75,000. Remember, it's not about taxable income — for example, the deeming rules will be applied to your financial assets. To reach this level of income from investments alone you would need a portfolio of around $3.3 million. Of course the income test looks at all sources of income, not just from investments, but as each income class is treated differently it can be complex.

The basic daily fee *can* be negotiated with your home care package provider — the income-tested care fee generally *cannot*. This is calculated by the government and used to offset the funding they provide on a dollar for dollar basis. Negotiating the basic daily fee might be a good idea: many home care package providers are quite willing to waive this.

At your ACAT assessment, the team will often recommend services. You are best to start researching providers early, as before your package can start you will need to nominate your provider. In the first edition of *Downsizing Made Simple* we highlighted the serious implications choosing the wrong home care provider could have on the amount of care you end up receiving. The 2018–2020 Royal Commission into Aged Care Quality and Safety has heard numerous stories of exorbitant administration fees, outrageous case management fees and inflated service charges. Rachel has seen a level 4 home care package with an administration fee of 52%! That means that a $51,000-a-year package would equate to just $24,500 of actual care, after fees.

Administration and case management are essential services: without them the package doesn't operate. But they are also largely invisible, making it difficult to know what is really involved and easy for unscrupulous operators to gouge their customers.

Changes introduced on 1 January 2023 cap the amount home care package providers can charge for managing your package at 15% and cap care management fees at 20%, so 35% in total. In addition, providers are not allowed to charge a package management fee in a month where no services (with the exception of care management) are provided, except in the first month. They have also been banned from charging for third party services through brokerage, handling or subcontracting fees.

Interim packages

As we explained earlier, often someone approved for a level 3 or 4 package is offered a level 1 or 2 package as an interim measure until a package at their approved level becomes available. Be wary of this: at the lower levels of home care package many people report receiving less care and support than they are able to access through CHSP, due to the administration, case management and travel fees in home care packages. So, accepting the package may mean you receive less care than you would for the same amount of money spent privately on care, especially for self-funded retirees. We explore this further below.

TABLE 21: Cost comparison — interim level 2 home care package v private care, self-funded retiree, at 1 July 2023

	Home care package	Private care
Basic daily fee	$11.87/day	—
Income-tested care fee	$35.95/day	—
Total user contribution	**$17,454/year**	**$17,454/year**
Home care package funding	$11.87/day (basic daily fee) + $49.49/day (basic subsidy)	$0
Total package funds	**$61.36/day or $22,396/year**	**$47.82/day or $17,454/year**
Package fees	$6,719 (30%)	$0
Funds for care	$15,677	$17,454/year
Hourly rate	$60	$50
Hours of care per year	**261 hours**	**349 hours**

Even if we assume that the cost of care through the home care package is the same as private care, there is still a $1,777 year benefit of using private care over a home care package. Of course, the figures will be different for a level 3 or 4 package, because the amount you can pay only increases slightly, but the funding the government provides doubles or triples.

Getting value for money

If your home care package provider charges an administration fee based on a percentage of your home care package funds, negotiating this down and instead spending that money on private services may give you more bang for your buck.

Look at it like this: the basic daily fee is roughly $84 per week. Let's say your provider is charging you 30% — the amount of buying power you have left is around $59 per week. Some people might say that it's not a significant difference. But often people save up their home care package funds inside their package because they know they have an operation coming up and they will need extra care to recover, or they want to buy a mobility scooter or have modifications made to their home and they need the funds to accrue. In such cases, saving that basic daily fee outside your package (where it is not charged a 30% fee) rather than inside your package (where it is), would mean the difference, over a full year, of $1,300. We call that significant money. In such a case, it is well worth trying to negotiate your basic daily fee to $0.

Make sure you understand how much you are paying and what you are getting for it — unfortunately, many people simply compare the amount they pay from their own pocket with the services they receive. If your contribution is zero, because you have a low income and the provider has waived your basic daily fee, what you get will automatically seem good value. But to assess the real value for money, look at the value of the whole package, which is a combination of what you pay and what the government pays.

Let's look at home care package funding — the funding amounts in *Table 22* are per person per day, and they work on a "plus plus" model, so it's the basic subsidy plus some or all of the additional subsidies and supplements, based on your care needs. Then in *Table 23* we look at an example.

TABLE 22: *Home care package funding, at 1 July 2023*

Package level	Basic subsidy	Dementia supplement
Level 1	$28.14	$3.24
Level 2	$49.49	$5.69
Level 3	$107.70	$12.39
Level 4	$163.27	$18.78
Oxygen supplement		$13.62
Enteral feeding supplement — Bolus		$21.58
Enteral feeding supplement — Non-Bolus		$24.24

TABLE 23: *Home care package example — full pensioner receiving level 3 home care package plus dementia supplement, at 1 July 2023*

		per day	per week
Your contribution	Basic daily fee	$12.20	$85.40
Government contribution	Basic subsidy	$107.70	$753.90
	Dementia supplement	$12.39	$86.73
	Oxygen supplement	$0	
	Enteral feeding supplement	$0	
Total package funds		**$132.29**	**$926.03**

You can see how easy it would be think, "Well, I only pay $85 a week and I get seven hours a week of care so I'm not getting ripped off". But if you look at the total value of the package, that seven hours of care is costing $926 a week. Is it worth $132 a hour?

You're in charge

Since July 2015, home care packages have been delivered on a consumer-directed care (CDC) basis. In principle, CDC gives choice to care recipients about the type of care and services they receive and who provides those services.

So, on to meal preparation. Can your provider do our favourite dish: Bushtucker hotpot with fluffy mash?

Since 27 February 2017, packages have been allocated to the care recipient (you). This means that you choose a home care provider to "host" your package, and that you can change providers if you are not happy with the service you are receiving. Home care packages are transportable nationally, so if you move, the package moves with you.

You control the allocation of funds across the range of care and services available within the package. You can also nominate the person or service provider you wish to use and the amount you wish to receive. For example, if you need physiotherapy you may wish to continue with your usual physiotherapist, but fund it from your home care package. Your home care package provider will contract your nominated physio to provide services, and arrange payment from the funding allocated to them by the government.

When selecting a provider to host your home care package, it pays to shop around. Consider too, that your preferred provider may not be able to take you on immediately. Some providers may have lower package fees, and make their profit by building a package using carers and services provided by their own employees. Others provide independent advice and choice. They work with you to build a personalised care plan, and then find services in your local community to deliver on that plan. If you don't like the carer or service they suggest, they'll change it for you — though of course the person or organisation must meet the criteria to provide home care services.

If you can't — or don't want to — be involved in managing your package, someone will need to do it for you. If that is the home care provider, naturally there will be a fee. But there are a few services that enable you to self-manage your package.

Self-managed packages

Choosing a provider that supports self-managed packages could save you a lot of money, while also giving you more say in who provides your care and when. They still develop a care plan for you and charge an administration fee, but it can be significantly cheaper, which means that more of the money in your package can be spent on care.

Remember, though, that case management and administration is not all about pricing and paperwork: a good case manager will know what care can be covered by a home care package and connect you with good quality services, so you don't have to do all the research yourself.

TABLE 24: Home care package service examples

What you can get	What you can't get
Personal services: assistance with bathing, showering, toileting, dressing, mobility and communication	**Personal expenses:** utilities, groceries, petrol, etc.
Nutrition: preparing meals, including special diets for health, religious, cultural or other reasons, assistance with eating	**Accommodation expenses:** mortgage payments, rent, etc.
Mobility: crutches, walking frames, mechanical devices for lifting, bed rails, slide sheets, sheepskins, tri-pillows, pressure-relieving mattresses and assistance using these aids	**Holidays:** flights, accommodation, etc.
Transport and personal assistance: shopping, visiting health practitioners and attending social activities	**Entertainment:** club memberships, tickets to sporting events, gambling, etc.
Nursing, allied health and therapy services: speech therapy, podiatry, occupational or physiotherapy services and hearing and vision services	**Other government-funded care costs:** CHSP, DVA services, or things covered by Medicare or the Pharmaceutical Benefits Scheme (PBS)

What you can get	What you can't get
Telehealth and assistive technology: video conferencing, digital technology (including remote monitoring), devices that assist with mobility, communication or personal safety, and classes to teach you how to operate your new tech	

If you can't manage the package yourself, a family member may be able to do it for you. After all, it may mean that rather than working longer hours to provide "top up" funds for your package, they can spend time with you doing the things you both enjoy.

Let's look at a couple of examples. "Let's get care" offers a self-managed package with fees of 18%, which covers basic services such as government compliance, paying your service providers, and keeping track of your package funds. You then need to identify your service providers, but there are online tools, like "Mable" for example, that connect individual support workers with people needing care in their local area. Mable charges up to 17.95% for their service (7.95% paid by you and 10% by the worker), which includes ensuring that support workers have a valid police check, are appropriately qualified or hold specific certifications if providing personal care or nursing services, and gives access to a comprehensive suite of insurances, and an incidents and complaints handling process, should any issues arise.

Self-managing your home care package, like self-managing your superannuation, is definitely not for everyone. While it may enable you to save some money and give you greater choice and control, with that comes responsibilities. Let's face it, if the provider isn't doing the work, then you are. Do you have the time, skills and confidence to self-manage your package? Ultimately you will be responsible for choosing your carers, and for negotiating days, times and pay rates — and if they go on holidays, are sick, or decide to quit, you will need find an alternative provider.

Let's look at the financial difference self-managing can make.

TABLE 25: *Cost comparison — self-managed v managed home care package, level 3, at 1 July 2023*

	Self-managed package	Home care package
Level 3 home care package $39,310/year		
Package fees	$7,076 (18%)	$11,793 (30%)
Package funds for care	$32,234	$27,517
Carer hourly rate	$50/hour	$60/hour
Hours of care per week	12 h 30 min	8 h 30 min

Tracey: Self-managing three home care packages

Being able to choose our own carers is brilliant — it's the greatest thing about self-managing.

Home care package management can be a little bit scary at first. I started with my dad's, which gave me the confidence to do my mum's, but I was hesitant with my step dad's, because his care needs were more complex.

Tracey and her mum

With Mum and my step dad the catalyst, ironically, was their front door. Their home care provider had quoted $6,000 to install a new door and level the floor so the wheelchair could get in and out. But the first door they went to install was too short, the glass panels on the side enabled anyone at the front door to look straight through to the bedroom, and there was no security screen! We ended up keeping the existing door and spending $150 at Bunnings for a little ramp that enabled the wheelchair to go over the lip. While all of this was happening, I was wondering about the bathroom door: it was much narrower, so the wheelchair couldn't even fit through the opening.

When I spoke to the HCP provider and said that I was thinking about taking over the management of the package, they were very happy for me to do it …. but said the same fees would apply! That just seemed crazy.

My step dad was getting day respite, but after a stay in hospital he came home with a level 4 package, which was only covering three showers per week. Everything was so expensive!

So I looked into my mum's package and discovered there was a 27% admin fee, plus other fees for this and that … I did the numbers and worked out that of the $15,000 government funding Mum had in her package, she was only going to get about $9,700 of care. All the rest was going in fees, plus there was a $500 exit fee. Luckily, I worked this out quickly and cancelled the package within 24 hours, so they waived the exit fee. But I still don't see why they need to charge an exit fee at all.

I'm still learning, but the care provider I use now, Avita, are great — they give me the information and guidance I need to manage the packages. A key benefit of self-managing is that we have more control. They put me on to a great company for home modifications — when they modified the bathroom they wanted to install grab rails, but what we needed was for the floor to ceiling pole to be put back in, so that's what they did.

Managing three packages can be hard: I have my own health issues and sometimes I get distracted and lose track. I have a book to keep track of appointments and a spreadsheet to keep track of payments. Each month I work out the number of days and the funding that's available for care and then I work out the ins and outs. I know that our provider does their payments on a Friday, so if I can get my part done by Friday morning the services will be paid that day.

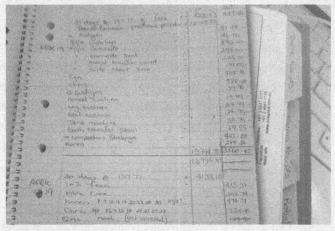

How Tracey manages the three home care packages

It's easy for my dad, as his services are very regular. For Mum and my step dad we have had a few one-off expenses like modifying the front door and bathroom, but now that we are in more of a groove it is much simpler.

By self-managing I can see exactly what is going in and out, and what money is left in the package — so when we need extra care I know if there is money there to cover that. Every now and then something isn't quite right, but because I can see that, we can get it fixed quickly.

Being able to choose our own carers is brilliant — it's the greatest thing about self-managing. We interviewed them as a family and chose the workers that fit with us. We showed them around, explained what we wanted done … it's tailored to us. We have built terrific rapport with our carers — they're like part of the family now.

We know who is coming and when too; with the old package we just didn't know who was coming — some of the carers were great but others we didn't really click with. They would give us a two-hour window for arrival, but we didn't really know when they were coming. Now we know exactly, and if they're running late, they send us a message.

In the beginning it's quite daunting — you think "Where do I start?" "What can I claim?" — but that's where having a good provider has been terrific. We have been able to get an app on my phone so I can see Dad and talk to him, and he can talk back to me. This means I can check in with him, and the home care package covers his internet. I mean, who would have thought that we could have that level of technology?!

The advice I would give is: go ahead and do it. It's not that hard. It's more daunting to think about than it is to do.

15

SHORT TERM SERVICES

While CHSP and home care packages are designed to assist people with ongoing care needs, several short term services exist to keep you out of long term care. These are primarily rehabilitation services that are aimed at getting you back on your feet after an accident or illness, and enabling you to stay at home longer. We discuss the major three services below.

Short Term Restorative Care (STRC)

STRC is an eight-week program aimed at slowing or reversing functional decline so that you can maintain your independence. Functional decline is when you have trouble doing everyday tasks such as showering, dressing, shopping, or driving. The program is designed to help you avoid residential aged care. You may receive your support in your home, in an aged care facility or in a combination of settings over the eight-week program.

There will be at least three health professionals responsible for overseeing your STRC program, one of which must be a doctor (normally your GP). The services you receive will be guided by your health care team and may include occupational therapy, nursing support, physiotherapy, personal care, technologies and minor home modifications.

Like other government-funded aged care services, to receive STRC you will first need to have your care needs assessed by ACAT.

If you are approved for STRC you will have six months in which to find a service provider and start receiving care. But don't leave it to the last minute: there may be a delay before you can start receiving care; the service you want may not be available in your area; or there may be a waiting list.

If you need to wait, you can receive CHSP services in the meantime, but if you start receiving other funded care — such as a home care package, or move into residential aged care — your approval will lapse.

The amount you pay towards your STRC will depend on where you receive your care. The maximum fee for care at home, as at 20 September 2023, is the basic daily fee of $12.53 per day, but in an aged care facility the maximum fee will be $60.86 per day. The government provides funding of just over $244 per day on top of your contribution.

STRC is very affordable, as there is no means-tested contribution: you just pay the basic daily fee. Of course, like other forms of care, if the basic daily fee is going to put you under financial pressure you should speak to your provider, who may agree to reduce or waive this fee. The role of STRC is to provide intensive care for a short period to help you get back on your feet (mentally or physically) and avoid long term care.

The STRC will become part of Support at Home from the 2025 financial year.

Transition Care Programme (TCP)

Transition Care Programme is similar to STRC in that the aim is to keep you out of residential aged care. Care through TCP may be delivered in a hospital, aged care facility or your own home. Like STRC, if you can afford to do so you will be expected to pay the basic daily fee towards the costs.

The key differences between the two are that TCP begins immediately after a hospital stay (or a "hospital in the home" stay). The ACAT assessment happens while you are in hospital, and you go straight into the TCP.

TCP runs for 12 weeks, with a possible extension for a further six weeks. If you were receiving government-funded care through a home care package or residential aged care facility before entering the TCP, your place in that service will be held for you while you complete the TCP.

Like STRC, TCP will become part of Support at Home from the 2025 financial year.

Respite services

Respite enables you to have a short term, funded stay in an aged care facility. You can have up to nine weeks each financial year. Respite is an excellent service, designed primarily to give carers a much-needed break, but it can also enable you to see what an aged care facility is really like.

A short stay — a couple of weeks is normally enough — in an aged care facility will give you a good sense of the meals, activities, other residents, staff and, most importantly, the care.

At the end of your stay, you may decide you love it and want to move in, or you may decide to go home wiser for the stay. Respite is not limited to a designated facility; you may choose to use it to try a few different facilities or have all of your stays in the same one — it's up to you and of course dependent on the availability of respite at the facility. You should be aware that Christmas is a particularly busy time and some families book months in advance; if you are looking to have a respite stay around this time it can pay to plan ahead.

So what does a respite stay cost? You just pay the basic daily fee of $61 per day — there is no accommodation payment and no means-tested care fee in respite. Naturally, if you want extras, such as beer or wine with meals, there may be an additional fee for that.

16

RESIDENTIAL AGED CARE

As you can see, there are a lot of different care services out there to help keep you well, or get you back on your feet and living as independently as possible. Understanding what you can access, the eligibility requirements and what the services cost will help you navigate the maze efficiently if that time comes.

When you are downsizing, it is important to understand that your home environment can play a key role in your ability to get the care you need. So even if you don't need care today, ask yourself: "How would this place work if I needed care?" This question will help you to look at your prospective new home through a different lens. For some people this just may be the key factor that helps them decide whether to go with option A or B.

In this chapter, we set out the basics of how residential aged care works, so you have a high level understanding of what the costs are and how the means testing works, so you can consider them as part of your future planning.

We must stress that aged care funding is complex; it is well worth seeking professional help from a financial planner who specialises in this area. The choices you make about how to fund the cost of care can have wide-ranging effects ... on pension entitlement, the cost of care itself, your ability to afford care in the longer term and the amount of money left to your estate. But most importantly, the choice you make should suit you, and ensure access to the care you need throughout your life.

A great many of us firmly announce that we have no intention of moving into an aged care facility. "An old people's home? Not me!" But the fact is that more than one third of men and half of all women who reach the age of 65 will at some time live in aged care. And very often, when they take the time to investigate their options, they are pleasantly surprised.

Many aged care homes today are more like hotels than the "old age home" of years ago. In fact, it is not uncommon for residents to comment to their children about "what a lovely hotel they are staying in" and "how friendly and helpful the staff are" while on a respite stay in an aged care home.

Before you can move into an aged care home you will need to be approved by an ACAT. In addition to an ACAT Assessment, there is another assessment process you may have to go through before or shortly after entering aged care: an income and assets assessment. The means test is not compulsory, however, you will likely find that some aged care facilities prefer new residents to have an assessment before they move in.

Understanding the outcome of the means test before completing it is crucial. We cannot emphasise this too highly.

Aged care means testing

Your assessable income and assets will determine whether you are eligible to be a low means resident, in which case some or all of your accommodation costs will be met by the government, or whether you are a market price payer, and the amount of any means-tested care fee you need to contribute. Most people pay the market price for their accommodation.

The good news is that the government uses a single formula, the bad news is that the formula can be quite tricky to calculate:

- 50c per dollar of income above $32,331/year (single) or $31,707 (couple, each) +
- 17.5% of assets between $58,500 and $197,735 +
- 1% of asset between $197,735 and $476,206 +
- 2% of assets above $476,206.

Where the outcome of the test is less than $67 per day you are classified as a low means resident and the calculated amount is the maximum amount you can contribute towards your cost of accommodation. Where it is more than $67, you are not eligible to be a low means resident and will need to pay the market price of your aged care accommodation. The calculated amount above $67 per day is the maximum means-tested care fee you will pay. For example, if your calculated amount was $85 per day, this would make you a market price payer, and your means-tested care fee would be $18 per day ($85 minus $67).

Assessable assets and income for aged care are broadly the same as your assessable assets and income for pension purposes and your assessable income includes your pension. If you are a member of a couple (including same sex couples) half of the total assets and income will be considered yours.

However, there are a couple of key differences. One is the treatment of your home, which is included in your assessable assets, up to a capped value of $197,735. It is exempt if a protected person is living there. The other is any amount you pay as a refundable accommodation deposit (RAD), which is included in your aged care assets.

The government uses the means testing arrangements to offset their funding. Basically, whatever you pay reduces the amount of funding the government pays the facility by the same amount. The facility cannot get more money from you than they would have received from the government. So even if your means-tested care fee was calculated, based on your income and assets, as $150 per day, if they were only going to receive $100 per day in funding the amount you could pay would be capped at $100 per day.

While the means test is carried out when you enter the aged care home to determine if you are a low means resident or market price payer, it is not a one-off assessment. The means test is recalculated quarterly to determine how much you pay. While you won't change from being a low means resident to being a market price payer or vice versa, the amount you pay per day can change significantly. It is not uncommon for low means residents to move into aged care paying a small accommodation contribution (or none at all) and at some point have to start paying the maximum amount of $67 per day, plus a means-tested care fee, because there is no longer a protected person living in the home and/or the house has been sold.

The cost of aged care

While means testing is a crucial element it does not calculate your cost of aged care. What it will cost you to live in aged care is far broader. You can break it down into your accommodation, your care, any extras and your personal expenses.

Your accommodation

If under the means test you are classified as a low means resident then your accommodation cost will be the means-tested amount. For example, if you are a full pensioner with $100,000 of assessable assets then the means-tested amount would be $20 per day, this would be your daily accommodation contribution (DAC).

If, like most people, you need to pay the market price for your accommodation then the price will be the amount you negotiate with the aged care home. The average price of aged care beds is currently around $450,000, but prices can go as high as $3 million if your bed has a view of the Sydney Harbour Bridge!

Whether you are a low means resident or pay the market price it is up to you whether you pay for your accommodation by a lump sum (known as a refundable accommodation deposit or RAD), a daily accommodation payment (DAP) or a combination of those two things, even including having your daily payment deducted from your lump sum.

The aged care interest rate (known as the maximum permissible interest rate or MPIR) is used to calculate the equivalent lump sums and daily payments. The aged care interest from 1 October 2023 – 31 December 2023 is 8.15% per year.

If you are a low means resident, your daily payment is calculated under the means test and the aged care interest rate provides the equivalent lump sum. So using the example above, if your daily accommodation contribution is $20 then your equivalent lump sum (using the current interest rate of 8.15%) would be $89,571. As you can probably see, the problem with this formula is that you don't have enough assets to pay that amount as a lump sum without risking running out of money, but you might choose to pay $50,000, which would leave $8.84 to be paid by daily payment.

If you are a market price payer, it is a little more straightforward. Your lump sum is the amount agreed with the aged care home, and any amount that you don't pay as a RAD you pay by daily payment using the aged care interest rate. For example, if your RAD was $550,000 and you chose to pay $200,000, that would leave $350,000 to be paid by daily payment of $78 ($350,000 x 8.15% divided by 365).

So that's your accommodation component, now let's look at what you pay towards your care.

Your care

Every resident pays the basic daily fee, which covers meals, laundry, insurances … the basics. It is set at 85% of the age pension, currently $61 per day.

On top of the basic daily fee is your means-tested care fee, which is calculated based on your assets and income each quarter. If your means change and as a result your means-tested care fee goes up your new amount starts from the next quarter (i.e. you won't incur a debt) but if the opposite happens and your means-tested care fee goes down as a result of a significant change to your assets or income (or both) during the quarter then you can accrue a credit. That's why you should always keep Centrelink up to date on any significant changes within 14 days of the change.

As we discussed earlier, your means-tested care fee is used to offset the government funding for your care, so it is limited to your cost of care. There are also annual and lifetime limits that apply. The annual limit is currently $32,719 and the lifetime limit (which includes any amount that you have paid as an income-tested care fee in a home care package) is currently $78,525.

Any extras

Many aged care homes offer you more than the legislated care and services and charge an extra or additional service fee for this. Common examples of additional services include Foxtel (or other entertainment services), a choice of meals, wine/beer with meals, and hairdressing.

The additional services are often packaged up so that the aged care home achieves economies of scale — while that can help keep the price low, it doesn't matter how low the price is if you're not using the service! So look at the package of services and make sure that you are going to use what you are paying for: hairdressing, for example, is not much use to you if you're bald.

Your personal expenses

While most of your living costs will be covered by the fees and charges you pay to your aged care home you will still have your own personal expenses to meet. Common costs include doctors' and specialist appointments, medications, clothing, Christmas and birthday presents for kids, grand-kids, and if you're lucky enough great grandkids; you may also have private health insurance costs. If you still have your former home, there will usually be a raft of expenses associated with that — from rates, land tax and insurance (check your insurance policy still covers you if your home is unoccupied for more than 30 days), real estate agent fees and any repairs and maintenance.

Many people hear the words "means tested" and jump to the conclusion that moving into an aged care home is affordable, only to find that the cost is far greater than their income.

CONCLUSION

Downsizing can be the start of a new and exciting chapter in your life. Remember, it is not about giving up or missing out on the things you have loved for years; it's about moving to a new stage in your life.

There are many options out there, and we have tried to give plenty of detail and case studies in this book, so you can choose your own adventure. Once you are aware of the options, you are much better placed to investigate in detail the ones that feel like a good fit for you.

No matter what your downsizing decision — strata development, granny flat, collaborative housing or retirement community — there will be legal and financial considerations. Remember to look at your rights, responsibilities, and costs — considering ingoing costs as you move to your new home, ongoing costs while you are living there, and outgoing costs you may incur if and when you leave.

Downsizing your home can mean supersizing your investments — which can affect how much income you will receive and your pension entitlement. So get good advice, choose your investments with an understanding of their different implications, and consider whether to use the superannuation downsizer contribution.

While you are at it, cover all your bases with some forward planning. Make sure your estate planning is in order, and documents such as your will, enduring power of attorney and advanced health directive are properly signed, witnessed, and accessible to the people who will need them.

If you intend your new home to be the one in which you will spend the rest of your life, make sure it will be suitable for home care in the future. As we discussed, there are a range of services to help you stay at home and in your community for as long as possible. While these services are home delivered, there are eligibility criteria and often long waiting times. So take action to arrange support sooner rather than later.

And if you think you may need a higher level of care, that too is best thought of now. There are contract options that can support a transition to higher levels of residential care, so why not plan ahead and choose one of those?

It is often said that moving from one home to another can be one of the most stressful experiences in your life. Our wish for you is that this book will relieve much of the stress that could occur, so your next move is your best move. Here's to the next stage of your life.

GLOSSARY

Aged Care Assessment Team (ACAT): The assessment required to access government-funded aged care services. In Victoria, it is known as Aged Care Assessment Service (ACAS).

Aged Care Quality and Safety Commission: The Commonwealth Government body responsible for accrediting, assessing and monitoring compliance of aged care service providers and resolving complaints.

Basic Daily Fee: The fee all home care package recipients can be asked to pay. There are four levels corresponding to the level of home care package. The maximum is set at 17.5% of the age pension.

Binding death benefit nomination: A way to override superannuation trustee discretion by directing the trustee who is to receive your superannuation benefit in the event of your death.

Body corporate: *Also known as an Owner's Corporation.* The managing body that deals with common ownership aspects of a multi-unit property. Its role is to manage compliance, insurance and essential services related to the building and common areas. Owners must abide by the body corporate rules (or by-laws). Each owner becomes a member on purchase, and pays a regular levy to cover the ongoing costs.

Capital gain/loss: The difference between the purchase price and sale price of an asset.

Commonwealth Home Support Programme (CHSP): Entry-level home support through services such as domestic assistance, personal care, social support, transport, and meals. CHSP is accessed through a Regional Assessment Service (RAS) assessment arranged through My Aged Care.

Day Therapy Centre (DTC): provides a range of rehabilitation and care services such as physiotherapy, speech therapy, occupational therapy and podiatry. Some transitional care services may also be provided.

Deeming: Calculation of income from financial investments (bank accounts, shares, managed funds, etc.) by Centrelink/DVA, which is not based on actual income but on rates set by the Commonwealth Government.

Deferred Management Fee (DMF): A fee designed to be paid on exit from a retirement village (and some land lease communities), enabling residents to pay a smaller amount on entry. The DMF typically forms the largest component of the exit fee. It is normally calculated using a percentage of the purchase or sale price and length of time lived in the village, up to a maximum period. *See also Exit fee.*

Deprived asset: *See Gifting.*

Entry contribution: The amount payable on entry to a retirement village, or in establishing a granny flat, where the contract doesn't give the resident title, but gives them the right to live there, typically in a leasehold or licence arrangement.

Exit fee: The sum of fees payable on exit from a retirement community. The DMF, if applicable, is usually the largest component. It may also include a share of capital gain/loss, marketing fees and sales commissions, and costs for refurbishment. *See also Deferred Management Fund (DMF).*

General service charge: Paid by all residents of a retirement village to cover ongoing operating costs, such as staff wages, lighting, cleaning and maintenance of communal facilities, insurances, and monitoring and maintenance of emergency call systems. Also called a recurrent charge.

Gifting: Centrelink limits the amount pensioners can give away at less than market value to $10,000 per financial year and no more than $30,000 in five years. Gifts in excess of the allowed amounts are assessable as assets and deemed to earn income for five years.

Income-tested care fee: A daily fee based on assessable income, which contributes toward the cost of a home care package. Full pensioners do not pay this fee; part pensioners have a cap of $6,544 a year; self-funded retirees have a cap of $13,087 a year; and a lifetime cap of $78,525 applies to all recipients. The fee is payable at 50¢ per dollar of income in excess of the threshold (equivalent to the full pension plus allowable income).

Independent Living Unit (ILU): Many retirement villages offer two levels of accommodation: ILUs provide the lowest level of care and support and are often little different to living in your own home, however there is likely to be an emergency call bell. *See also Supported Living Units.*

Land lease community: A purpose-built community for people over a certain age (generally 50), where residents own their home and rent the land from the operator. This rent is commonly referred to as site fees.

Long term maintenance fund: The fund used by retirement village operators to cover the cost of replacing or repairing common areas and buildings. In a strata title development (whether a retirement village or not) a similar fund is often known as a "sinking fund". *See also Body corporate.*

Owners corporation: *See Body corporate.*

Pet friendly: A property that allows residents to keep pets. Approval of the pet is normally required, with the intention of ensuring that both the pet and the residents will be safe and happy.

Pooled lifetime income stream: A type of annuity that pays a regular sum during your lifetime, and then to a reversionary beneficiary, if nominated. Your money is pooled with other peoples' to support the ongoing payments.

Refundable Accommodation Deposit (RAD): A lump sum accommodation payment to an aged care facility. Return of the RAD is guaranteed by the government.

Refurbishment cost: The cost of returning your home to an agreed standard on departure from a retirement village. The standard is normally specified in your contract. "Refurbishment" typically means bringing the home up to the same standard as new homes in the village, so if you have lived in the village for a long time this could mean substantial works. "Reinstatement" typically means returning the home to its original condition, which may require repairing any damage, steam-cleaning carpets and some repainting. In a land lease community or strata title development, the level of works you undertake, and their cost, is normally at your discretion.

Respite stay: A short stay in an aged care facility, up to 63 days per financial year. The basic daily fee applies.

Retirement village: A purpose-built community for people over a certain age (generally 55), which operates under the *Retirement Villages Act* in the state or territory.

Serviced apartment: *See Supported Living Units.*

Short Term Restorative Care (STRC): An eight-week customised program of care and services tailored to a person's specific needs to re-establish independence and reduce the likelihood of needing long term care.

Sinking fund: *See Long term maintenance fund* and *Body corporate.*

Site fees: *See Land lease community.*

Supported Living Units (SLU): Many retirement villages offer two levels of accommodation: SLUs provide care and support, such as cleaning, laundry, changing linen, meals and may include care services. May include some care services. They are sometimes called serviced apartments. *See also Independent living units.*

Transition care: Short term care provided immediately after a hospital stay to assist a person to continue living in their own home. Can be provided in a hospital, aged care facility, community centre or at home. Accessed through an ACAT assessment.

Veterans' Home Care (VHC): A service providing care to eligible veterans and war widow/ers in a home setting. Services can include personal care, domestic assistance, home and garden maintenance and respite care. Accessed through a Veterans' Home Care assessment.

DIRECTORY

AGENT SELECT is an independent expert in comparing and appointing the top performing Real Estate Agents for property sales. They can help negotiate fees and can often organise for all marketing costs to be paid at settlement. Selling a home can be complicated, stressful and expensive, but Agent Select helps guide you through the whole process, at no extra cost.

☎ 1300 040 463 | ✉ info@agentselect.com.au | ↖ *www.agentselect.com.au*

AVEO owns, operates and manages 94 retirement communities across Australia, offering a wide range of living choices. Aveo's care services cover the full spectrum from independent living to aged care, including palliative, dementia, respite and home care.

☎ 13 28 36 | ↖ *www.aveo.com.au*

BOLTON CLARKE is Australia's largest independent, not-for-profit aged care provider. They offer at-home support, retirement living and residential aged care. With RSL Care Queensland and the Royal District Nursing Service Victoria at the heart of Bolton Clarke they have been caring for Australians since 1885.

☎ 1300 22 11 22 | ↖ *www.boltonclarke.com.au*

CANSTAR is a financial comparison site that researches and rates products across more than 30 different categories, including banking, insurance, superannuation and investments. Their findings are displayed in comparison tables to help you find the products that best suit you. Companion site Canstar Blue compiles research customer satisfaction in more than 120 consumer product categories. Canstar is authorised to provide general advice only; they are not accredited to provide advice or recommendations about specific circumstances or requirements.

✉ enquiries@canstar.com.au | ❦ *www.canstar.com.au*

CARE CONNECT is one of Australia's largest not-for profit home care specialists. Their aged care services include home care packages, Commonwealth Home Support Programmes and community packages (ComPacks) across New South Wales, Victoria and Queensland. They aim to enable older Australians to live independently at home in safety, with support and connection with family, friends, and community.

📞 1800 692 464 | ❦ *www.careconnect.org.au*

CENTRELINK is the Australian Government body that administers all social security payments, including the age pension. They are also responsible for conducting the means testing for home care packages and residential aged care for pensioners and self-funded retirees.

📞 13 27 17 | ❦ *www.centrelink.gov.au*

CHALLENGER LIFE is a multi-award-winning life insurance company with $23 billion in assets under management as at 30 June 2023. They are Australia's largest provider of annuities.

☎ 13 35 66 | 🖰 *www.challenger.com.au*

COLLABORATIVE HOUSING is a web guide to collaborative living options in Australia, developed by University of Technology Sydney's Institute for Sustainable Futures. The site offers information about various models of collaborative housing, stories from people who have established or moved into collaborative housing, and explanations of design, legal, management, and financial considerations.

🖰 *www.collaborativehousing.org.au*

COMMON EQUITY NSW (CENSW) is a registered housing provider and peak body for rental housing cooperatives in New South Wales. To be considered for a CENSW waiting list, individuals must be eligible for social or affordable housing and then meet individual co-operatives' criteria. CENSW also supports the establishment and development of independent co-operatives (for example, co-operatives looking to jointly purchase their own properties) on a fee-for-service basis.

🖰 *www.commonequity.com.au*

CONNECTNOW arranges utility connections at your new address on your behalf. The service is free to consumers.

☎ 1300 554 323 | ✉ info@connectnow.com.au |
🖰 *www.connectnow.com.au*

DEPARTMENT OF VETERAN'S AFFAIRS (DVA) provides a range of programs and income support payments to assist the veteran and defence force communities. They provide a range of in-home and community support programs to assist ex-services personnel and war widows and widowers to continue living independently.

📞 *(metro)* 133 254 *or (regional)* 1800 555 254 or *Veterans' Home Care (VHC) assessments* 1300 550 450 | ✉ GeneralEnquiries@dva.gov.au | 🖊 *www.dva.gov.au*

DOWNSIZER gives homebuyers a solution to purchase their next home with zero cash deposit by using their Downsizer Bond. All the buyer needs is sufficient equity in their existing home to qualify. Payment for the new home happens in full at the time of settlement.

📞 1800 788 996 | 🖊 *www.downsizer.com*

FINDER is a comparison site with a broad brief. Their staff research and compare products in more than 100 categories — from broadband to business loans; credit cards to cruises; and health insurance to headphones. These services are free to consumers, with revenue earned from advertising and referral fees.

🖊 *www.finder.com.au*

FUNKY LITTLE SHACK was born from the desperate need in the market for more sustainable and affordable living options for families that also offer contemporary, stylish living. Created by Mel Miller, with a Masters in Architecture, she is passionate about living bigger through bringing more freedom and sustainability to living, including social and financial sustainability, and firmly believes 'downsizing does not have to mean downgrading'.

Funky Little Shack offers a full design service and utilises local (FLS licensed) builders across Australia for quality construction which normally takes just 8–12 weeks.

📞 1300 377 744 | ✉ info@funkylittleshack.com.au |
🐦 *www.funkylittleshack.com.au*

GEMLIFE is a developer of premium over-50s lifestyle resorts. With a focus on high quality, active and engaged living, GemLife delivers first-class recreational and leisure facilities through its award-winning country club concept, and its meticulously designed, modern and stylish homes.

📞 1800 317 393 | 🐦 *www.gemlife.com.au*

INGENIA COMMUNITIES offers housing options for independent seniors.

Ingenia Connect is a free service helping residents navigate care programs and services as their needs change, which promotes wellbeing and long term independence.

Ingenia Lifestyle's innovative land lease model allows over 55's to buy their own brand new home, lease the land with no stamp duty and no exit fees, and keep 100% of any capital growth.

Ingenia Lifestyle
📞 1800 135 010 | 🐦 *www.ingenialifestyle.com.au*

Ingenia Gardens are affordable senior's rental communities providing flexibility and peace of mind for like-minded seniors to enjoy a rewarding and peaceful retirement.

Ingenia Gardens
📞 1800 44 54 64 | 🐦 *www.ingeniagardens.com.au*

IRT GROUP is a community-owned operator of 35 retirement communities and home care service hubs across New South Wales, Queensland and the Australian Capital Territory.

📞 134 478 | 🖋 *www.irt.org.au*

KEYTON (Formerly Lendlease) is a leading owner and operator of senior living communities in Australia. Over more than 30 years, they have developed and operated more than 75 villages nationally, for 17,000 residents across the country.

📞 1800 550 550 | 🖋 *www.keyton.com.au*

LAND LEASE HOME LOANS was formed to give residents and prospective residents of a land lease community or manufactured home estate (MHE) with similar financing opportunities to those available to traditional house and land homeowners. At time of writing, they are the only financier in the market that offers a home loan secured by a home in a land lease community.

📞 1300 555 626 | 🖋 *www.landleasehomeloans.com.au*

LDK HEALTHCARE develops and operates seniors' living villages where older Australians can age in place in the comfort of their own home. LDK's vision is for every senior Australian to be treated with love, decency and kindness in their ageing journey.

📞 1300 535 000 | 🖋 *www.ldk.com.au*

LENDLEASE – *see Keyton*

LET'S GET CARE is a self-managed, government-approved home care provider, which aims to give every home care package holder control of their care services to support their independent living. Let's Get Care charges a low flat fee, and offers clients access to a large pool of services Australia wide.

☎ 1300 497 442 | ✎ *www.letsgetcare.com.au*

LEVANDE operates 58 retirement communities across Qld, NSW, Vic, SA and the ACT, caring for about 11,000 residents. Levande was established in 2022 to operate the portfolio on behalf of EQT, a European investment fund that bought the properties formerly owned by Stockland.

☎ 1800 72 71 70 | ✎ *www.levande.com.au*

LIVING CHOICE has been creating stunning retirement communities in premium locations since 1992, offering a wide choice of homes, facilities and services. Their award-winning over 55 communities are located across NSW, QLD and SA.

✎ *www.livingchoice.com.au*

LOCAL AGENT FINDER helps you search, compare and connect with local real estate sales agents. Finding the right agent can make a big difference to the sale price or rental return of your property, as well as how stressful the process is. This service helps you identify the right person for the job.

☎ 133 033 | ✎ *www.localagentfinder.com.au*

MABLE is an online platform that enables you to find and connect directly to local, approved independent care and support workers.

☎ 1300 73 65 73 | ✉ info@mable.com.au |
🏹 *www. mable.com.au*

MY AGED CARE is the Australian Government's gateway for the Commonwealth Home Support Programme (CHSP), home care packages, short term care programs, respite care and residential aged care. It provides information on types of aged care services, eligibility and costs, including fee estimators, and coordinates referrals to the Regional Assessment Service (RAS) or Aged Care Assessment Team/Service (ACAT/ACAS), who will then contact you regarding an assessment.

☎ 1800 200 422 | 🏹 *www.myagedcare.gov.au*

NARARA ECOVILLAGE aims to create a sustainable ecovillage that is stylish, inter-generational, promotes good health, and achieves "triple bottom line" (social, financial and environmental) outcomes. The eco village is in development and welcomes new members.

🏹 *www.nararaecovillage.com*

NIGHTINGALE HOUSING is an independent not-for-profit organisation creating homes that are socially, financially and environmentally sustainable. Nightingale believes homes should be built for people, not profit.

✉ info@nightingalehousing.org |
🏹 *www.nightingalehousing.org*

ODYSSEY is a new, innovative player in the senior living space, offering a full range of care, and resort-style living with activities and restaurants. Their first village is at Robina on the Gold Coast, and their second village is opening soon at Chevron Island on the Gold Coast.

📞 07 5551 6720 | 🦅 *www.ohg.net.au*

REAL ESTATE AUSTRALIA (REA GROUP) is the single largest online real estate advertising portal in Australia. Their services now include suburb reports, assistance engaging sales agents, and other support services for buyers, sellers, and renters.

🦅 *www.realestate.com.au*

REGIONAL ASSESSMENT SERVICE (RAS)
see My Aged Care.

RETIREMENT LIVING COUNCIL is the national leadership group of the retirement living sector, championing policies that deliver more senior Australians age-friendly homes and services in retirement communities. They operate ARVAS, the Australian Retirement Village Accreditation Scheme — an independent accreditation scheme for retirement communities, launched in 2019. ARVAS contains standards relating to all elements of a resident's experience, including community participation, dispute resolution, entry and exit. ARVAS-accredited villages are audited against all of these standards, providing peace of mind to current and potential residents about the quality of service they provide.

📞 07 3225 3000 |
✉ retirementliving@propertycouncil.com.au |
🦅 *www.awisemove.com.au*

RYMAN HEALTHCARE owns, and operates 46 retirement villages across Victoria and New Zealand. Ryman villages operate a "continuum of care model", in which independent living and serviced apartments are co-located with full aged care services, including low care, high care, specialist dementia care, and home care packages provided by Ryman.

☎ 1800 288 299 | ✎ *www.rymanhealthcare.com.au*

STOCKLAND *– see Levande*

UNITING have 24 independent living villages across NSW and the ACT, with homes for every lifestyle and budget for seniors over 70. Uniting's extensive range of services supports seniors to live an active, social and independent life in addition to providing care as their needs change.

☎ 1800 864 846 | ✎ *www.uniting.org*

VICTORIAN BUILDING AUTHORITY offers resources for consumers about combustible cladding — just remember the rules for rectification are different in each state and territory.

✎ *www.vba.vic.gov.au/cladding*

Unbiased information available at your fingertips

Visit our website

Download resources
Use the calculators
Read articles

DownsizingMadeSimple.com.au

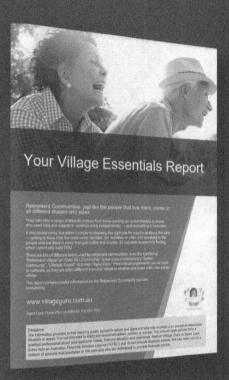

A **Village Guru Report** shows you
the costs of moving to, living in,
and leaving a village, together with
estimates of your age pension and
rent assistance entitlements.
It can compare up to three options
side-by-side so you can make your
move with confidence.

Find a village
that can offer you a
FREE Village Guru Report

DownsizingMadeSimple.com.au/
find-a-village/

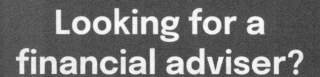